More Team-Building Activities for Every Group

By Alanna Jones

Rec Room Publishing

PO Box 404
Richland, WA 99352
(509)946-7315

ISBN 0-9662341-7-0

A special thanks to my friends at the
Columbia Challenge Ropes Course for
their creative ideas, insight and friendship.

Contents

Disclaimer

The games in this book are designed to be fun and interactive. Common sense should be used when leading and/or participating in these games, and safety for all those involved should be considered. The author and publisher are not responsible for any actions taken by any person/s who leads and/or participates in any of the games or activities in this book.

So have fun, be safe, know the limits of the members of your group, and always give people the choice of participation to insure a good time for all!

Introduction

Team-building is becoming so popular that it is becoming harder and harder to find games that haven't already been played by someone in the group. Some games you can do over and over again, but team-building challenges are often more effective if they are new to everyone in the group. This is why I have written the book *More Team-Building Activities for Every Group* — to provide an additional 107 games to your team-building library. With this book and *Team-Building Activities for Every Group*, you will have 214 games to give you fresh ideas for every group you lead.

Although the games in this book are all new and different from those in the first book, they cover the same aspects of team-building with games to "Mix It Up," "Stir It Up," "Team Up," and "Open Up." The "Mix It Up" games help people get to know each other better; "Stir It Up" games help them to feel more comfortable around each other. "Team Up" games build trust, teamwork, communication, and "Open Up" games pave the way for them to affirm one another and to share more deeply with one another. These are the stages of team-building that every group needs to go through in order to become a solid, cohesive group.

In the "Mix It Up" chapter the games are designed to help people learn more about one another, to get people talking with all the members of the group, and to create a comfort level for everyone involved. These games are fun, lighthearted, and can be played with any group, no matter how long the people have been together.

The games in the "Stir It Up" chapter are just-for-fun games that are sometimes a bit crazier than the "Mix It Up" games, allowing people the chance to laugh as a group, act crazy, be loud and to have fun. These types of games can cause a group of people to bond more than before. It can also knock down walls and open up the group to being more willing to take on challenges that come along when working as a team during the "Team Up" activities.

The "Team Up" games are designed to challenge a group of people to work together to complete a task, solve a problem, or to do both while always working as a group. Some of the games require the group to be split into teams that compete against one another. The competition creates an added incentive for groups to accomplish a task or finish a challenge. Plus, it often makes the game more fun and provides the chance for good debriefing when competitive attitudes arise. There are also many games that simply require a group to work together, and the competitive games can often be altered so that one team challenges itself to reach a goal or to simply finish. With or without the competitive aspect groups will easily find an activity in the "Team Up" chapter that will challenge any team.

Once a team has spent time working together the group members are often more willing to open up and share about themselves or to share about the dynamics of the group. The activities in the "Open Up" chapter give people the opportunity to share in a nonthreatening manner through the activity itself. Some of the activities are geared towards affirming one another. Other activities focus on the attributes and strengths of the group. When a group spends any amount of time together and bonding occurs, it is a good idea to give people the chance to share how they feel about each other, themselves, and about the group as a whole. This will put closure on the time spent together and give people the opportunity to learn more about themselves as a result of their time spent with the group. This time can also help team members feel more like valued members of the group and be willing to participate more.

As in the first book, the "Team Up" and "Open Up" chapters contain Discussion Prompts at the end of each activity to act as a guide for the debrief that should take place at the end of each game. The discussion at the end of the activity is a key factor in creating a team-building experience for the entire group. It is the part of the game where most of the learning takes place. When people share what they got out of the activity, what they observed, and why they felt the way they did, then everyone can learn more about themselves and about the dynamics of the group. When a group is successful the discussion often affirms the positive traits of each group member and brings to light the strengths of the group as whole. When a group struggles to complete a challenge and individuals become frustrated, the discussion is a chance for group members to learn from the experience and to apply their understanding to future tasks. Any activity that is meant to be a learning experience will benefit from a discussion at the end.

Often, the best discussions take place halfway through an activity. If a group can stop, look at what is going wrong, and regroup, then they have the opportunity to turn any failure into a success by talking, communicating, and not giving up. Please note that the Discussion Prompts are meant to be a guide, but things will often take place during an activity that need to be addressed or that can be learned from. The prompts do not focus on those unpredictable issues. Sometimes the prompts provided will deal with what role each person had in the group or on what actually happened. Other times they will focus on how the activity was similar to real life and draw parallels for the group to think about. Whatever the case, a good discussion can often turn a simple activity into a valuable learning experience.

When leading team-building games you have the opportunity to be very creative and to add to the experience by presenting the activity in a fun and unique way. Many of the challenges require the group to work together to get from point A to point B or to complete a task successfully. If you start the game by presenting the group with a creative story about why they have to complete the task, it can be more fun for the team and can loosen up the atmosphere as well. Your story can be as crazy as you want to make it or it can be a parallel to something the group is working on.

If the group is going to be doing a series of activities, you can create a map that they have to follow and have each activity be a point on the map for them to get through until they finally make it to the "shore of success." When using a map you can combine the story telling with a visual. Another idea you might want to try when doing a series of games is to give the group a clue to what their next activity will be after they accomplish each task. The group must work together to figure out where to go and what to do. Once the team arrives at an activity you may have the directions written out rather than verbally giving them to them. There are lots of ways to present each game in a fun and unique way.

Within the four chapters of this book are activities that build a group of people into a team. By starting with simple games that allow people to share with one another you'll set the stage for the group to become more comfortable with one another. After this you can move on to games that create a sense of belonging by getting people to laugh and be crazy with one another. The team-building games will challenge your group and help them grow, develop, and become more confident. Once you have done all this you will be ready for times of deeper sharing.

All types of groups can use the games in this book to bond, grow, and learn more about one another. Whatever type of group you work with you will find team-building games fun, interactive, and a favorite part of any group time.

Mix It Up

Team Thumb O' War

Objective

To mix up the people in the group, for people to share about themselves with others, and for people to get to know more about one another.

Group Size

8 or more

Materials

➲ List of questions (found on the following page)

Description

Break the group into two teams, and have the teams line up facing one another. Each team member's opponent will be the person directly across from them. Before each round of "Thumb O' War," give the group a question each player must answer to their opponent after introducing themselves. After all players are finished sharing, the "Thumb O' War" begins. It is played like this:

Each player cups the fingers of their right hand into a C shape, curving their fingers around their opponents fingers, holding thumbs up. They then move their thumbs over, under and around each other while chanting "One, two, three, four, I declare a Thumb O' War." Then say "shake," and "shake" thumbs as thought the thumbs are shaking hands. Next, they say, "Go!" and each player tries to trap the other players thumb under his/her own thumb for the count of three without letting go of hands, thus winning the round.

After each round take a count of how many people beat their opponent on each team and award a point to the team with the most wins. One team has the person in the front of the line go to the end and everyone moves down one so each person is facing a new partner for round two. Continue for several rounds giving people the chance to meet and share with a number of people in the group.

Thumb O' War Questions

1. What is one thing you got for Christmas?
2. Who is your favorite relative and why?
3. What do you plan to do tomorrow?
4. What is your favorite thing to surf for on the Internet?
5. Where would you like to go for your next vacation?
6. What is your favorite season and why?
7. What was your favorite birthday you have ever had and why?
8. Who is your favorite music group or singer?
9. What would be your ultimate dream job?
10. What is your favorite thing about this group?

Group "Newlywed" Game

Objective
To learn more about select individuals and to generate interaction among group members.

Group Size
6 or more

Materials
- A stack of 3x5 cards
- Pens or pencils
- Two copies of your questions for each team

Description
This game is similar in format to the old "Newlywed" game that used to be on TV.

Break the group into two or more teams of up to eight people each. Each team selects the one person in the group that they think they know the most about and sends them out of the room. Give the individuals who were selected the list of questions (found on the next page or make up your own) and ten 3x5 cards and a pen or pencil. Give their team members the same materials. Set a time limit, and instruct the teams to answer the questions as they think their teammate in the other room will answer for him/herself putting each answer on a separate 3x5 card with its corresponding number on the opposite side of the card. The cards should then be stacked in order, number side up, with 1 on the top and 10 on the bottom of the pile. The people who left the room should do the same, making sure to answer the questions truthfully.

Next, ask the people who left he room to return and sit up front. Send one representative from each team to join them with the cards from his/her team. Ask the first question and have the person who left the room hold up his/her card with the answer they gave, and have their team member do the same. If the answers match the team gets a point. Do this for each group, and for all the questions, and the team with the most points at the end is declared the winner.

Group "Newlywed" Game Questions

1. Favorite Movie
2. Shoe Size
3. Favorite Place to shop
4. Favorite Cereal
5. Mom's first name is…
6. Usual bedtime is…
7. Color of toothbrush is…
8. Furthest place traveled to this summer was…
9. Food had for lunch today…
10. Color of car you came here in today…

Group Top 10 List

Objective
To promote group interaction and to make group members feel more comfortable with one another.

Group Size
4 or more

Materials
- Paper
- Pens or pencils

Description
Break the group into teams and give each group a piece of paper and pen or pencil and a time limit. Each group must create a "top 10" list of things that go with the category you give them, or ask them to think up categories of their own. Or, you may ask each group to come up with a title for a top 10 list and then pass it to another group who must complete the list. After the time limit have one person from each group read the list that their group came up with.

Some List Title Ideas
1. Top 10 reasons you would want to live in this city…
2. Top 10 reasons you would want to work at this company…
3. Top 10 reasons you would want to go to this school…
4. Top 10 reasons this group should not give a singing performance…
5. Top 10 reasons people should listen to the leader of this group…

Discussion Gift

Objective
To learn more about one another, to increase group interaction, and to have fun.

Group Size
6 or more

Materials
- A gift
- Wrapping paper
- Tape
- Questions written down on paper

Description
Select a gift that can be shared among the group (i.e., a bag of candy) and wrap it in many layers of paper with lots of tape. On each layer write a question, or tape one on that is written on paper. Each person takes a turn opening a layer of paper and must answer the question that is revealed when they unwrap their layer.

Make sure there are enough questions and layers of paper for each person in the group to answer one question.

The last question should be "If you get to the gift will you share it with the group? Why or why not?" Then allow the last person to choose whether or not to share the gift.

If your group is large, you may want to break them into smaller groups for this activity.

Learn With Legos®

Objective
For group members to learn more about one another and to increase interaction among group members.

Group Size
8 or more

Materials
➲ A large tub of Lego® building blocks
➲ A list of characteristics (found on the following page)

Description
   Prior to the activity build a structure out of Legos® that each team must try to duplicate. Make sure that you have enough of each piece used in the sculpture for each group to duplicate the sculpture out of the remaining pieces.

   Place the sculpture somewhere in the room that is far away from where the groups are working but in a place where they can easily go and look at it at any time. Break the group into teams and explain to them that they are to try and duplicate the sculpture, but they must first win each piece. Each team is seated together and has no Legos® to start with, but they may send one person to look at the sculpture at any time.

   The leader then calls out a characteristic (see list on opposite page) and each team sends up one person from their group who best fits that description. When all the team representatives are with the leader, they must decide who wins that category (i.e. person with longest hair, youngest, etc.) and that person gets to choose two Lego® pieces while everyone else may only choose one.

   Team members then take the Lego® piece back to their team and try to build the Lego® sculpture piece by piece. If someone gets a Lego® piece they can't use, that is their loss. Also, if someone is not seated with their team (if they are up looking at the sculpture), they may not go up for the characteristic that was called while they were gone. The first team to exactly duplicate the sculpture (color, size, and position of each piece must match exactly) wins!

Characteristic List

1. Longest hair
2. Youngest
3. Born the farthest away
4. Longest last name
5. Biggest shoe size
6. Lives the closest to this place
7. Has been on the most vacations in the last year
8. Has the most full siblings
9. Birthday closest to today
10. Shortest person
11. Most body piercings
12. Has the youngest baby brother or sister
13. Has the most traffic tickets
14. Has been a member of this group for the longest
15. Newest member of the group
16. Has been to the most foreign countries
17. Shortest hair
18. Spent the most money today
19. Has played on the most sports teams
20. Can do the most one-armed push-ups

Candy Bar Story

Objective
For people to begin to feel comfortable around one another, and for everyone to give input when in a group discussion.

Group Size
4 or more

Materials
- A variety of candy bars or candy in their wrappers
- Tag board
- Tape
- Markers

Description
Divide the group into teams and give each team a mixed bag of candy bars or wrapped candies. Try to pick candies with unique names (i.e., $100,000 Bar®, Snickers®, Nerds®, etc.). Instruct the teams to write a story about themselves on the tag board using the names of the candies in their story and taping the candy onto the board where it goes. When all the stories are finished, have each team read theirs to the group, then allow them to eat the candy.

Balloon Questions

Objective

For group members to learn more about one another in a fun, interactive way.

Group Size

4 or more

Materials

- Balloons
- Paper
- Pens or pencils

Description

Give each person a balloon and a small strip of paper. Ask them to write down a question on the slip of paper and place it in their balloon, then blow the balloon up and tie it. Once everyone has finished, instruct the group to hit their balloons into the air, trying to keep all the balloons in the air for as long as possible.

After a few seconds tell everyone to grab any balloon and sit in a circle. Each person takes a turn popping his/her balloon and then answering the question. For small groups you may have each person in the group answer every question.

Do You Have My Puzzle?

Objective
To mix up the people in the group and to help them interact outside their usual relationships.

Group Size
8 or more

Materials
➲ Paper
➲ Colored markers
➲ Scissors

Description
Break the group into teams of four or more and give each group a piece of paper, colored markers and scissors. Give each group an assignment of your choice (i.e., to write a note, answer a question, or draw a picture), with the one requirement being to fill the entire page. Then have them cut the paper into puzzle pieces, with one piece per team member.

When everyone has a puzzle piece, have them walk around the room and mingle. When you say so, each person should find someone to trade puzzle pieces with. You may have them trade with a specific person (i.e., someone who was born in the same month as you, someone who has the same eye color, etc.). You may have them trade several times with different people.

When the trading is finished, instruct everyone to find the rest of the people who have the puzzle pieces that go with their piece and to put this puzzle together as a group. If there is a question on their puzzle they should answer it within their group or come up with a group answer to share with the large group.

My Adjectives

Objective

For group members to become acquainted with each other in a different way.

Group Size

6 or more

Materials

- ➲ 3x5 cards
- ➲ Marking pen
- ➲ Music source

Description

Prior to the activity make a pile of 3x5 cards with an adjective written on each one. Try to use as many different adjectives as possible.

Gather the group together and give three of the adjective cards to each person. Start playing some music and instruct the group members to go around the group and exchange cards with others until they are satisfied they have found three adjectives to describe themselves. Once a person has found three adjectives they are happy with they should sit down. You may need to have a few extra cards in a pile that people can trade with at the end if they haven't been able to find cards they were satisfied with.

When everyone is seated allow time for group members to share the cards they have and to explain why they chose those adjectives.

Airplane Battle

Objective
For group members to share about themselves with the rest of the group in a fun and nonthreatening way.

Group Size
6 or more

Materials
➲ Paper
➲ Pens or pencils

Description
Prior to the activity make up a list of questions that each person must answer about him/herself.

Give everyone a copy of the questions and a pen or pencil and ask them to fill out their questionnaire. After each person has finished answering their questions ask them to make a paper airplane out of this paper. (You may want to do this all together and instruct them how to make a plane so that they all look the same.)

Once all the planes are made divide the group into two teams and put one team on each side of the room with a line down the middle. On the "go" signal each team tries to get as many airplanes as possible across the line to the other side before you say "stop." The team with the fewest airplanes on their side wins. You may do several rounds of this and give a point after each round.

After the "airplane battle" ask each person to pick up one airplane and to then sit in a circle. Have group members take turns reading the paper they ended up with. You may have other group members guess whose paper is being read or read them anonymously or simply have them tell whose paper it is that they are reading.

Variation

➲ Have each person write down a question that the person who gets their plane must answer or that the group members must answer.

Pennies for People

Objective
For group members to share about themselves and to get to know more about each other at the same time.

Group Size
4 or more

Materials
- A large jar of pennies (25 per person plus extras)
- 3x5 cards
- Pen or pencil

Description
Prior to the activity make a pile of action cards (see sample ideas below). Gather the group into a circle. If you have a large group you may want to have more than one circle of up to 20 people. Give each person 25 pennies and place a pile of cards in the middle of the group along with the penny jar full of remaining pennies.

Each person in the group takes a turn selecting a card from the pile and reading it out loud. At this point the person who selected the card must do what it says and either gain or lose a penny. You may have everyone in the group follow the directions on the card or just the person who selected the card.

Card Ideas
1. If you have been to Mexico – take a penny from the pot
2. If you have pierced ears – give a penny to the person on your left
3. If you like to drink coffee – give a penny to each person in the group
4. If you know how to ride a unicycle – take a penny from the person across from you
5. If you have seen all of the Star Wars movies – take a penny from the person on your right

6. If you are the oldest child in your family – give a penny to the person of your choice
7. If you rode your bike this last week – give a penny to the pot
8. If you have had pizza in the last week – take a penny from a person of your choice
9. If you were born on an odd number day and in an odd number month – Give a penny to the person across from you
10. If you like spicy food – take a penny from the person you talked to last

Variation
➲ Give each person a blank card prior to the activity and give them some sample card ideas. Then ask everyone to make a card for the game and put them all into the pile and then play the game with these cards.

I'll Trade Ya!

Objective

For group members to interact with one another and to create an atmosphere that is fun and comfortable for everyone.

Group Size

8 or more

Materials

➲ Small colored candies, (i.e., M&M®'s, Skittles®, Spree®, Starburst®, etc.)

Description

Give each person the same number of pieces of candy. Each person starts with a mixture of colors and is trying to get all one color of this candy. Group members must trade pieces of candy with each other in attempt to get all of one color. They may only trade one piece at a time and may not trade with the same person twice.

Instruct group members to share something about themselves (i.e. your favorite kind of candy, why you are here, etc.) with each person they trade with. Once a person has all one color they are allowed to eat their candy.

Variation

➲ Instead of using one kind of candy that has different colors, use a wide variety of candies and each person tries to get all of the same kind of candy.

Find Your Friend

Objective

For group members to learn more about one another and to learn what others in the group already know about them.

Group Size

6 or more

Materials

- ○ Sticky-type name tags
- ○ Marker
- ○ 3x5 cards
- ○ Pens or pencils

Description

Place a sticky name tag on the back of each person in the group with the name of another group member on it. Do not tell them whose name is on their back.

Give each person a 3x5 card and a pen or pencil and instruct group members to find out as much as they can about the person whose name is on their back and to write this information down. While gathering information each person tries to guess whose name is on his/her back. After a set time limit, gather the group together and give each person a chance to guess whose name they had on their back. After guessing, or after others have to reveal it to them, each person should introduce the person whose name they had by using the information gathered on their card.

Whose Shoes?

Objective
To interact with others in the group and to make decisions as a group based on what they already know about each other.

Group Size
10 or more

Materials
➲ Paper
➲ Pens or pencils
➲ Optional: two large baskets or boxes

Description
   As people come into the meeting, have them take off their shoes, tie them together, and place them in one of two boxes, baskets or piles. Make sure that each pile has an equal number of shoes in it.

   Once the meeting starts ask the participants to sit in one section of the room if they put their shoes into pile "A" and to sit in another section of the room if their shoes are in pile "B". Give each group two pieces of paper and a pen or pencil. Have the two piles of shoes in front of you and hold up one pair at a time. For each pair of shoes you hold up one team must guess whose shoes they are (the team whose shoes are not in that pile) and write it on a piece of paper. The other team must write down whose shoes they actually are. Both teams should number their papers. If people don't know everyone's name they may guess whose shoes they are by describing what the person is wearing, etc.

   After all the shoe guessing has taken place you may collect the lists and see how many each team answered correctly, or you may have them read their answer list to each other and check their own sheet.

Variation
➲ For very large groups you may have four teams with two teams paired up to guess each other's shoes.

Mix It Up

Interview Competition

Objective
To get people to talk with one another and to get to know more about one another while playing a game.

Group Size
10 or more

Materials
- 1 copy of question list per person (see ideas on next page)
- 1 name tag per person
- Pens or pencils

Description
Give each person a list of questions and a pen or pencil, and a name tag. Have them complete their question sheet but tell them not to show it to anyone.

Ask group members to pair up with a partner and give them one minute to find out as much information as they can about each other by asking questions found on the sheet. People may not show each other their sheet at this time, they may only ask them the questions on it. After the minute is up, ask the group two or three of the questions and see who can remember what his/her partner said. If they remember correctly, they get one point and mark it on their name tag. Do several rounds of this and see who has the most points at the end of the game.

Question List Ideas

1. Your birthday?
2. Your shoe size?
3. Your favorite vacation spot?
4. Best friend?
5. Favorite movie?
6. Job you would most like to have?
7. Favorite Saturday night activity?
8. Number of siblings?
9. Favorite snack food?
10. Name you would want for yourself if you could pick it?
11. Why you are here today?
12. Kind of car you came here in today?
13. What you did before you came here today?
14. What you hope to get out of being with this group?
15. Your goal in life for the next year?
16. Ideal boyfriend or girlfriend would be?
17. Favorite relative?
18. Person you most admire?
19. Favorite holiday?
20. Your biggest handicap?

Odd or Even

Objective
To mix up group members, to learn more about one another, and to have fun.

Group Size
6 or more

Materials
➲ Optional: Small stickers

Description
Ask group members to find a partner. Once everyone is paired up ask a question such as, "Who has the most siblings?" The questions should provide information but at the same time determine a "winner" in each pair. If there is a tie (i.e., both people have the same number of siblings) then the pair must do a round of "Rock, Paper, Scissors" to determine a winner. The winner gets to call "odd" or "even," and on the count of three both people hold out one or two fingers. If the total of the fingers held out is even, the person who had even for that round gets one point. The same goes for odd. After each round everyone must find a new partner and answer a new question that the leader gives to them to determine who calls "odd" or "even" for that round.

Small stickers may be used to keep track of points. Give each person ten (or any number) stickers and have them place them on the front of their shirt. After each round the loser must give a sticker to the winner. The person with the most points or stickers at the end of the game is declared the winner.

The questions posed may be light ("Whose birthday is closest to today") or deeper and more revealing ("Who has or had the highest GPA in school?"). Some questions may be based on opinion and the two people must argue their point ("Who has the hardest job?"). Base the questions on your group's needs and dynamics.

The Meaning of Your Name

Objective
To learn about one another by thinking of them in a new way.

Group Size
4 or more

Materials
➲ A book of names and their meanings (baby name books are helpful)

Description
If you know the names of several group members, prior to the activity, look them up in the book and write down their meanings. If you don't know who will be at the group meeting you will need to do it at the meeting. Read the meanings of one name at a time to the group and have members guess whose name goes with that meaning. Once you reveal the true name behind the meaning you may have group members or the individual whose name was called decide if the meaning is a good fit for that person or not.

Variation
➲ Prior to the activity, write up the meanings of the names of several group members and have individuals try to guess the name that goes with each meaning. You may have them work on this in groups as well.

More Team-Building Activities

Stir It Up

Bopper

Objective
To increase the comfort level in the group through fun, interactive play.

Group Size
10 or more

Materials
- Newspaper or foam "noodle" toy cut in half
- Tape
- Chairs

Description
Prior to the activity roll up some newspaper and tape them together, to make a long stick or "bopper" that isn't too hard. Or, you may use a foam "noodle" toy that has been cut in half.

Gather the group into a circle and have everyone sit in a chair. Going around the circle, have each person select one thing from a chosen category that becomes his/her identity for the game (for instance, a US state, a kind of fruit, a breakfast cereal or anything else that has enough items in it for each person to have a different name). Next, choose one person to stand in the middle and give him/her the "bopper."

The person in the middle calls the "name" of someone in the group (i.e., "Alabama") and whoever has that name must stand up, call another name, and sit down before the person in the middle bops them on the head. Each person must stand up when their "name" is called and quickly call another "name". Once a person is bopped on the head they move to the middle and the next round begins.

Variation

➲ This can also be used as a "get to know you" game for strangers using group members' real names.

Shuffle Your Buns

Objective
To play a fun game in which everyone is included.

Group Size
10 or more

Materials
➲ Chairs

Description
   Have group members sit in a chair in a circle and with one person standing in the middle. There should be one empty chair in the circle. The person in the middle is "it" and tries to sit in the empty chair. "It" says "left" or "right" and the circle must move one place in that direction. "It" tries sit in any empty chair. "It" may yell "left" or "right" at any time to make the group members switch directions. If the middle person gets into the chair then the person who should have been in the chair becomes "It" for the next round.

Give The Hat a Whack

Objective
To help group members become more comfortable with one another in a fun and physical game.

Group Size
4 or more

Materials
⊃ A pile of hats
⊃ Newspaper

Description
Prior to the activity gather as many different hats as you can or have group members make hats out of newspaper. Each person selects (or makes) a hat and puts it on. Give everyone one large sheet of newspaper and ask them to roll it up.

On the "go" signal everyone tries to knock off everyone else's hat with the rolled-up newspaper. Once a person's hat is knocked off they step to the side and enjoy the show. The last person with a hat on his/her head is declared the winner.

Variations
⊃ For a large group you may have many different rounds of this game with the winners from each round playing in a final match.
⊃ Using masking tape, tape a paper cup to the top of each hat and people try to knock the cup off of each other's hat.

Ground Volleyball

Objective
To help group members become more comfortable with one another.

Group Size
6 to 20 is ideal

Material
➲ Chairs
➲ String
➲ Beach ball or other soft ball

Description
In a large room or outside area set up a volleyball court with a low net by tying string between two chairs or placing a row of chairs across the middle to form a "net." Divide the group into two teams and have each team sit down on their side of the "net." Now, play a regular game of volleyball, except everyone must be sitting down for the entire game. Players may use their hands or even their feet to hit the ball and may scoot around the court on their bottoms. Rotate and serve as normal.

Clothespin Clip

Objective
To create an atmosphere that is fun and comfortable.

Group Size
6 to 20 is ideal

Materials
➲ One pair of dice
➲ A large bag of clothespins

Description
Gather the group into a circle with a large pile of clothespins in the middle. Pass the dice around the circle, take turns rolling. Whenever someone rolls seven they run to the middle and start clipping clothespins all over themselves as quickly as possible. (You may rule that they are not allowed to clip on the edge of their clothing to make it more challenging.) Meanwhile players keep rolling. As soon as someone else rolls a seven the person in the middle must sit back down in the circle while the next person clips as many clothespins on as possible. Continue in this manner until all the clothespins are gone. The person with the most clipped on at the end is declared the winner.

Variation
➲ Do this in pairs and have the person who rolls seven clip clothespins onto his/her partner. The winner may be the person with the fewest clothespins or the team with the most.

Baton Pass

Objective
To increase the comfort level of the group.

Group Size
4 or more

Materials
➲ Timer
➲ Small baton-like item

Description
  Ask for four volunteers to come to the front of the room and give one of them a baton-like item (a paper towel roll will work). Select a category such as: Disney® cartoon characters, breakfast cereals, kinds of candy with chocolate in them, NFL® teams, US states, names of people in this group, books of the Bible, etc. Once the category is given set a timer for about 30 seconds. The person holding the baton must name something in the category and pass the baton to the next person, who must do the same. Players may not name something that has already been said. When the person keeping time yells "stop," the person holding the baton is out and must sit down. Give the group a new category or let them continue with the same one. The last person left wins that round. You may play several rounds with different people.

Variation
➲ Have the group members say the words of the pledge of allegiance, a song, cheer, etc. The first person says the first word, the second person says the next word and so on down the line until someone makes a mistake.

Scrabble® Relay

Objective
For group members to work together in a fun, interactive, and competitive game to increase group interaction.

Group Size
8 or more

Materials
➲ Paper or 3x5 cards
➲ Marking pen
➲ Whistle or other noise-making devise (or a loud voice)

Description
Prior to the activity make a set of large Scrabble®-like tiles with a single letter and point value on each (use paper or 3x5 cards).

Divide the group into two or more teams of four or more members each. Give each team four random cards to start with and give them the following rules.

1. When the whistle blows your team may send someone up to the pile to select one card randomly.

2. The first team to make a complete word of five or more letters gets ten bonus points, plus the point value of the word (the total of all the points for each letter in the word)

3. The first team to make a six letter word gets ten bonus points plus the point value of the word, and so on for the first seven-eight-nine, etc., letter word.

4. After the final card has been taken, each team will have ten minutes to make a crossword-like arrangement out of your letters. You will get five points per word and ten bonus points if you have the most words. (Note to leader: you may or may not give word value points during this phase of the game).

Object Pass

Objective

For group members to laugh together and have fun during an interactive game.

Group Size

6 to 12 is ideal (large group may be broken into smaller groups)

Materials

➲ Varied

Description

At the beginning of the game ask each person to select an object of any size, get it, and stand in a circle with it. On the "go" signal each person must pass his/her object to the right and keep going in this pattern until an object is dropped. You may need to keep the objects flowing by saying "pass," "pass," "pass," etc. Once an object is dropped the person who dropped it (or the two people who dropped it) is out but the object stays in. The game continues with fewer people but the same amount of objects. Until there is only one person left — or until it become impossible and the remaining participants are all declared winners.

Sticker Tag

Objective
To mix up group members while playing a fun, fast-paced game.

Group Size
15 or more (more is better)

Materials
➲ Small stickers

Description
Place a small sticker on the back of each person who will be participating in the game. On the "go" signal each person tries to grab as many stickers as they can off of the backs of the other players. Once someone gets a sticker they place it on the front of their shirt and it cannot be grabbed by another player.

There are two winners at the end of this fun game. The last person to have a sticker on his/her back and the person who collected the most stickers can both be crowned Sticker Tag champions.

Team Telephone Ball

Objective

For group members to practice teamwork in a nonthreatening environment while playing a fun game.

Group Size

4 or more

Materials

- ➲ Old telephone books or old magazines
- ➲ 1 trash can, box or bucket

Description

Place a trash can, box or bucket in the middle of the room. Have the group get into pairs and link arms with their partner. Give each pair an old telephone book or old magazine and have them sit in chairs or on the floor. On the "go" signal each pair begins ripping out pages of their book, wadding them up and throwing them into the "basket," keeping track of how many baskets they make. Each person can only use his/her outside arm for this activity. After a time limit or after each team runs out of paper, stop the game and have each team announce how many points they have. For a faster clean up you may give points for each paper wad picked up off the floor and thrown into the basket after the initial game is finished.

Ground Tag

Objective

For group members to become more comfortable with one another by playing a fun, energetic game.

Group Size

16 or more (more is better)

Materials

➲ None

Description

Have the group get into pairs and tell all but one pair to lie face down on the ground in a large circle, facing in. There should be enough space in between each pair for two people to lie down. The one pair that is not lying down will be playing tag with one person "it" and the other being chased. The one being chased may lie down next to anyone at any time. This person stays down, but the partner of the person he/she laid down next to must get up and become the person being chased. Once someone is tagged they become it and chase the other person, who tries to get down next to someone for safety. Runners can't run across the circle, they can only run around the outside.

Train Wreck

Objective
To learn more about one another and to mix up the group while playing a fun, energetic game.

Group Size
12 or more (more is better)

Materials
➲ One chair per person, minus one

Description
Line the chairs up in at least two single file rows facing forward to resemble seats on a train. One person starts without a chair and goes to the front of the group and becomes the "conductor." The conductor says something about him/herself (i.e., "I like bubble gum ice cream"), and everyone who likes bubble gum ice cream must get out of his/her chair and move to a vacant chair. The conductor tries to find an empty seat as well. The person left without a place to sit becomes the new conductor. If at anytime the conductor yells "train wreck," everyone must get up and find a new seat.

Team Ball Tag

Objective

For group to begin to use teamwork in a nonthreatening, interactive game.

Group Size

6 or more (the more the better)

Materials

- ➲ Lots of small soft balls or rolled up socks (that can be used as balls), or paper wadded up into balls
- ➲ One blindfold for every two people

Description

This is a crazy, fun game that can be considered a team-building activity as well.

Divide the group into pairs and have each group decide on one person to be blindfolded first. After every group has blindfolded one member, toss out all the balls you have onto the floor. The blindfolded partner has to pick up the balls and try to hit other blindfolded participants with guidance from their partner. (You can decide on what type of guidance is allowed.) Once a team is hit three times they are "out" and must sit down. The last team standing wins the game.

More Team-Building Activities

Team Up

Lego® Instructions

Objective

For team members to work together while giving and following complex directions.

Group Size

4 or more

Materials

- Lego® building blocks
- Paper
- Pens or pencils

Description

Break the group into two or more teams of two to eight members each. Give each group a pile of Lego® building blocks, paper, and a pen or pencil. Instruct the teams to create a structure out of Legos® and then write down clear directions as to how to duplicate exactly the structure they have created. After each team has finished the task, they need to make sure no one can see their sculpture, but keep it intact.

Once all of the teams have a set of complete directions they must give them to another team who has to follow them exactly in order to attempt to duplicate the sculpture the original group created. (You may need to have an additional pile of Legos® for group members to use if they don't have enough in their pile.) Compare original Lego® creations with the ones made from the directions and see how close they are to each other at the end.

Discussion Prompts

1. Was it easy or difficult to create a structure as a group? Why?
2. Did you all agree on how the directions should be written?
3. Was it easy to follow the directions you were given? Why or why not?
4. Did one person do most of the work in your group or did everyone contribute equally? Is this how life usually is?
5. Were you happy with the end results?
6. What did this activity tell you about your team?

Variation

➲ Simply challenge the group to make one or more sculptures out of the Legos® given to them and to write down the directions for the sculptures. At a later date challenge the group to put together the sculptures based on the written directions.

Message Shred

Objective
To work together as a group to accomplish a goal.

Group Size
4 or more

Materials
- Paper
- Pens or pencils
- A paper shredder
- Tape

Description
Divide the group into teams of two or more members each. Give each group a piece of white paper and a pen or pencil and ask them to write a message on the paper. The message may be about something specific such as "things that tear our group apart" or "what we need to do in order to put it back together." Another idea is to ask each group to write a note to another group about the things they appreciate about them. Or you may have group members write down questions that another group has to answer.

Once each group has finished writing have them take their paper to a paper shredder and put it through. They should collect the pieces, put them into a pile, and give them to another group to put back together. Give each group a roll of tape for this portion of the activity. Once all the messages are put together have group members talk about the message they received.

Discussion Prompts

1. How did you come up with the message that you wrote?
2. How did you feel about the message you received?
3. What role did each person take on in your group for this activity? Was everyone involved?
4. Do you have anything in your life you wish you could shred? Why?

Bridge of Life

Objective
For team members to work cooperatively in decision-making and planning.

Group Size
4 or more

Materials
⊃ None

Description
Break the group into teams of four to ten. (This game may be played as a race or as a one-team challenge.) Mark off an area that is wider than all the team members standing side by side. The challenge is for each team to get one member from one side of the area to the other without touching the ground or being carried.

Some possible solutions are:
- for team members to lie down, forming a human bridge for the person to crawl across
- for the team to pass the person down the line in a prone position, with team members shifting position in line as necessary
- for the person to walk on the feet of his/her team members

Discussion Prompts
1. How did you decide who would be the person who had to try to get across?
2. How did you decide on a method for getting this person across?
3. Did everyone contribute to the decision process? Why or why not?
4. What role do you usually take when part of a decision-making process?
5. Do you wish you had a different role? Why or why not?

Variation

- ➲ Tell the group they have to get half of the team across rather than just one person.
- ➲ Simply challenge the entire group to get one person across a large open area.
- ➲ Put obstacles in the area that the group must get one person around when moving them from one side to another.

Team Tent Set Up

Objective
For one person to lead while the others rely on his/her leadership in order to accomplish a difficult task.

Group Size
5 to 10 is ideal

Materials
➲ One unassembled tent
➲ Blindfolds

Description
Select one person in the group to be the leader and blindfold everyone else. Give the group a tent to set up completely while blindfolded relying only on verbal directions given by the leader.

Discussion Prompts
1. How did you feel while blindfolded?
2. Did everyone have something to do the whole time?
3. How did you feel while you were waiting for directions? What did you do?
4. Do you ever get impatient while waiting for a leader to give you directions?
5. As the leader, how did you feel your team did?
6. How did you feel about your leadership role?
7. What are some ways you could do this activity more easily next time?

Variations
➲ You can do this type of activity with many different tasks for a group to do with one leader giving directions.
➲ Have more than one leader giving directions and see who listens to whom.

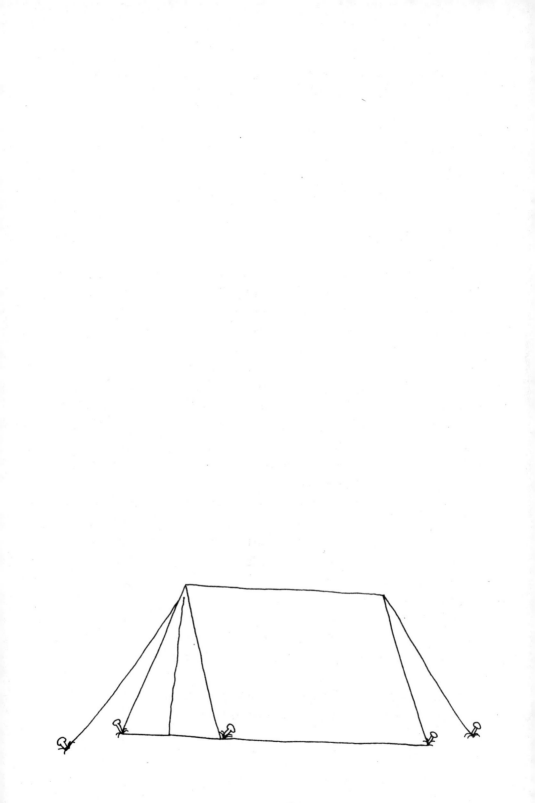

Turning Letters into Words

Objective

For group members to work together to accomplish a goal.

Group Size

8 or more

Materials

- ⊃ 3x5 index cards (about 5 per person)
- ⊃ Marking pens

Description

Divide the group into teams of four to ten and give each team the same number of 3x5 index cards. Ask them to divide the cards evenly among their group members. Give each person a marking pen and instruct them to write down any five letters of the alphabet on the cards (one per card) and to not show these letters to the other members of their team. After everyone has done this, have each team put all their cards into a pile.

Set a time limit (five to ten minutes) and challenge the teams to use their cards to make as many words as possible, using each card only once. You may give points according to how many words they come up with, extra points for longer words, etc. The team with the most points at the end wins.

Discussion Prompts

1. Did the letters you chose hurt or help the group? How did this make you feel?
2. Did the helpfulness of the letters you chose depend on the letters that others chose?
3. Do you sometimes do a lot of work for a group and then find out later it wasn't needed? How do you feel when this happens?

Variations

➲ After each team has made as many words as they can with their letters, have them write the words down on a list. Send the list and cards to another group, who can get bonus points for any additional words they make.

➲ Tell the participants why they are writing down letters before starting and then surprise them by telling them they have to give their pile to a different group.

➲ Let people collectively choose which letters to use and then either allow them to keep the cards or make them trade with another group.

➲ Simply challenge the entire group to make as many words as they can, with the letters they've chosen. Once they have done this, challenge them to make more words than before, still using the same letters.

Paper Tear

Objective
For team members to work together to accomplish a task.

Group Size
3 or more

Materials
- Colored construction paper
- White paper
- Glue

Description
Divide the group into teams of three to eight and give each person in the team a different colored sheet of construction paper (you may give more than one if there are more colors than people). Without explaining why, instruct the participants to tear their sheet into pieces and to put the pieces into a pile. It doesn't matter how many pieces each person tears.

Next, give each team a large sheet of white paper and some glue. Now each group must make a picture out of the torn pieces of paper without tearing them anymore. Each picture must be of something and not just a design. Ask each group to name their picture and then to share it with the group when they are finished.

Discussion Prompts
1. Would you have torn your paper differently if you had known you would be making a picture out of it?
2. Was it hard or easy for your group to make something out of the paper you had?
3. What makes your picture unique?
4. In what ways is your team unique?
5. How did everyone contribute to this project?
6. Does everyone on your team have a unique way of contributing to your team? How does this enhance your team?

Variation

➲ Challenge the group to use the torn paper to make a poster that represents the team.

Parade Float

Objective
To work together creatively as a group.

Group Size
5 or more

Materials
➲ Optional: Crepe paper, paper, newspaper, tape, string, chairs, aluminum foil, stuffed animals, etc.

Description
Break the group into teams of five or more. Each team must make a parade float out of themselves, with one team member riding on the float. This can be done without any props, but it is more fun if you supply a pile of objects and materials that they can use. After all of the floats are completed, hold a parade so that they can be shown off. You may have an awards ceremony afterwards and give each float a unique award.

Discussion Prompts
1. How did you get started? Did it take your team awhile or did you get going right away?
2. Is everyone happy with the float that their team created? Why or why not?
3. How do you feel about the teamwork that was used when making your float?
4. What are some ways that people can work together to complete a project in an effective and positive way? Did your team do this?

Variation

➲ Gather a few flatbed trailers and have each group make a float that is actually pulled by a car for the parade. Let each group go one at a time so the others can see their float, or have the parade be a giant circle.

➲ Use wheelbarrows for the floats to be made on, with one person riding in it.

➲ Have groups name their floats.

Minefield

Objective
For group members to think about problems the group has and come up with possible solutions.

Group Size
2 or more

Materials
- Paper
- Pens or pencils
- Blindfolds

Description
Give each person a piece of paper and pen or pencil. Ask everyone to think of things that they feel are disruptive to the group and write them down. (You may or may not have them share what they have written.) Everyone should then wad up their paper and throw it into a designated area on the floor. These are now the mines in the minefield.

Now have group members get into pairs. Blindfold one member of each pair, and have them try to cross the minefield without stepping on any of the mines while their partner verbally tells them where to go. You may have more than one person walking though the field at once, for an added challenge, have them walk towards one another.

Discussion Prompts
1. Would it have been easier to get to the other side without the mines in the way?
2. How did you overcome all of the mines in the minefield?
3. How can the team get past things that are disruptive to the team process?
4. Do you feel that this team does this? Why or why not?
5. What are some ways this team can eliminate the "mines"?

Variation

➲ The leader gathers all of the papers once they are complete and reads them to the group anonymously. He/she then wads each one up and throws it into the minefield.

Potato Head

Objective
For group members to work together to complete a project.

Group Size
2 or more

Materials
- One potato for each team
- One knife for each team
- Toothpicks
- Various fresh vegetables – celery, carrots, cucumbers, green beans, etc.

Description
   Break the group into teams of two or more and give each group a potato, toothpicks, a knife and various vegetables. Instruct the groups they are to make the most creative "Potato Head" they can. After each group has completed their Potato Head, have them share their creations with the rest of the group.

Discussion Prompts
1. What part did each person take in creating your Potato Head?
2. What does your potato say about your group?
3. Would your potato have been different if you had made it by yourself?
4. Is it OK for things to be different when you work with a group than when you work by yourself?

Variation
- Give each group several potatoes and have them make a potato sculpture of the group.
- Do this as one group rather than breaking into smaller teams.

Blanket Pull

Objective
For group members to rely on each other.

Group Size
3 or more

Materials
- ➲ Blanket/s
- ➲ Various objects to be used as obstacles
- ➲ Blindfolds

Description
This activity works best on a smooth floor such as tile or a gym floor.

Gather up one or more old blankets and give one to every three to five people, or have teams take turns. Blindfold all but one of the team members. Then place several obstacles (chairs, balls, mats, people, etc.) across the floor. The person who is not blindfolded rides on the blanket while those who are blindfolded pull him/her through the obstacle course. The person riding on the blanket gives verbal directions to those pulling him/her as to how to navigate through the course.

This can be done as a relay race, a timed event, or just for a fun challenge.

Discussion Prompts
1. How was trust a factor in this activity?
2. Did you trust your teammates? Why or why not?
3. Do you ever have to rely on others to guide you through life?
4. Do you ever have to guide others? Are you good at this?
5. How do you feel about your team's performance today?

Move the Water

Objective

For team members to solve a problem and then follow through with their solution.

Group Size

3 or more

Materials

- Paper cups
- Water
- Rubber bands
- String
- Scissors
- Various other materials: cardboard, paper, tape, etc.

Description

Break the group into teams of three to six. Give each team a paper cup that is full of water, a few rubber bands, some strong string, scissors, and a variety of other items. Tell them that they must move the cup of water from point A to point B. At NO time may anyone touch the cup of water with their hands, but they may use any of the supplies given to them to accomplish the task.

One possible solution: Cut the string into at least three pieces. Tie the pieces to a rubber band. Stretch the rubber band open by team members pulling on the string, and place it over the cup. Release tension to make it fit tightly around the cup (the rubber band may have to be doubled if it is large). Now have team members carefully help lift the cup by lifting their string and move it across the space.

Discussion Prompts

1. Was this activity easy or difficult for your team?
2. Did you find an obvious answer, or did you have to work at it?
3. When solving a problem as a part of a team, does it usually take awhile or is it usually a quick process?
4. What is the process a team should go though when solving a problem?

Variations

➲ Have teams pour the water into another container.
➲ Use confetti or some other lightweight items in the cup to make it easier to lift.
➲ After successfully using the rubber bands and string to lift the water, have the team do a "Cup Stack" by putting ten paper cups into a pyramid (see the book "Team-Building Activities for Every Group").

Stretcher Challenge

Objective
For team members to work together to accomplish a goal.

Group Size
7 or more

Materials
➲ Old sheets
➲ Various objects that can used as obstacles

Description
   Break the group into teams of seven to nine and give each group a sheet. Each group must select one person to ride in a "stretcher" that the group must make out of the sheet by rolling up the sides and holding onto it. Set up an obstacle course for the group to go through while carrying their person with things to go over and under, such as tables and chairs. You may time each group, do this as a race, or simply as a group challenge.

Discussion Prompts
1. How was trust a factor in this activity?
2. (For the person in the stretcher) How did you feel when your team was carrying you?
3. Was anything difficult about this activity?
4. Was everyone involved in carrying your teammate through the obstacle course?
5. How is trust a factor on any team that you are involved in?
6. Are you trustworthy?

Variations

➲ Give the group various materials such as long sticks, rope, sheets, etc., and ask them to decide how to make their own stretcher.

➲ If in a camp or outdoor setting with lots of natural materials available, have groups make a "stretcher" out of materials that they find.

Storyboard

Objective

For group members to work together on a presentation.

Group Size

4 or more

Materials

- A digital or Polaroid camera for each team
- Tag board
- Tape
- Marking pens

Description

Divide the group into teams of four or more. Give each team a camera that can produce instant pictures, a piece of tag board, tape and marking pens. Set a time limit and instruct the groups that they are to use pictures of their group to tell a complete story, with captions below each picture. When the time limit is up, have groups share their creation with the rest of the group.

Discussion Prompts

1. Did you feel comfortable being in front of a camera? Why or why not?
2. Did everyone have an equal role in deciding what should be done?
3. Did someone emerge as a "director"? Was this a good thing for your team?
4. Is it good for teams to have a "director," or is it better for everyone to have equal input?
5. How do most of your teams operate? With a director or not?
6. What role do you take on in most groups you participate in?

Variations

⮑ You may give the groups a story that they must make a storyboard of.

⮑ Each group makes up a story and gives it to another group, who must make a storyboard about it.

⮑ Do this activity with video cameras and have them take "still" pictures while someone else narrates each "scene" to create a video "storyboard".

Lego® Pair

Objective
For group members to communicate well in order to carry out a plan together.

Group Size
2 or more

Materials
➲ Lego® type building blocks

Description
Divide the group into teams of two or three and have them sit back to back. Give each person a pile of Legos®. Instruct them to have every member of their team build the exact same structure without looking at each other's work. They are to use the Legos® they have in front of them. If they need to share, they must do so without looking at each other's work. After a set time limit, allow team members to look at each other's work and to see how similar or different each one is based on how well they communicated with each other.

Discussion Prompts
1. How was communication a factor during this activity?
2. How well do you feel your group communicated with each other?
3. What happens when a group of people must work together but do not communicate?
4. Why is communication so important when working with others?
5. What is your communication style when working with a group? Is this effective? Why or why not?

One Dollar Challenge

Objective
To work together to creatively solve a problem and for everyone to be involved in the problem solving.

Group Size
4 or more

Materials
- $1 for each team
- Transportation for each team

Description
   Divide the group into teams of two to eight and give each team one dollar. Set a time limit and challenge the groups to go around town and buy as many things as they can, using only the dollar they have been given. Each team must return at the end of the time limit with a bag of items and the receipt for each item. The team with the most items wins. Teams must be creative for this challenge! For instance, they may ask if they can buy one french fry for one cent and get the cashier to give them a receipt. However, each team only gets one point for each item that they bring back (i.e., they can't bring back more than one french fry).

Discussion Prompts
1. Did your whole team agree on where to go? If so, why? If not, how did you deal with this?
2. Did each person have the same role each time you went to a store, or did different people do the talking at different stores? Why was this?
3. How hard is it to agree on things as a group? If you don't agree, do you usually say so? Why or why not?
4. Do you feel your team was successful at this challenge? Why or why not?

Poker Challenge

Objective
For a team of people to work together to gain an advantage over the other teams.

Group Size
10 or more

Materials
- ➲ Playing cards
- ➲ Various other objects

Description
Divide the groups into teams of five to ten members each. Announce different challenges that the groups must each try to accomplish in a given amount of time (i.e. build a pyramid, sing a commercial, do 100 collective push-ups as a team, etc.) Give each group a turn to accomplish the challenge, and if they do so, give them one playing card from a shuffled deck of cards. Each team should make sure that no one on the other teams can see their cards at any time.

After going through several challenges and handing out at least five playing cards to each group, instruct the teams to select their best five cards for a hand of poker. Each team sends up one player to the front with their five cards. Ask one team representative at a time to show their hand and see who the winner is.

Discussion Prompts
1. Was this game fair? Why or why not?
2. Did the best team really win? Why or why not?
3. What did your team have to do in order to have a better chance of winning this game? Did your team do this?

Variation

➲ Give each team a list of challenges and a time limit. For each challenge they accomplish they get one card, but they can do as many as possible during the time limit.

Shadow Charades

Objective
For a group of people to work together to give information to one person on their team.

Group Size
8 or more

Materials
- ➲ One large white sheet
- ➲ A slide projector, overhead projector, or other light source

Description
Hang one large sheet from the ceiling or walls at the front of the room. Place a light source such as a slide projector or overhead projector behind the sheet and direct the beam onto the sheet leaving room between the light source and the sheet for people to stand.

Divide the group into teams of four to seven. Ask one team to have all of its members go behind the sheet except for one. Give the group members behind the sheet something to act out by using their bodies to cast shadows on the sheet — no talking allowed. It should be something that would be hard for one person to act out by him/herself (i.e., a heard of elephants, someone ordering food at a drive-through, a football game, etc.). Have a list of things ready and give each team one minute to see how many things they can act out on the list with their teammate, who is on the other side, guessing what they are. Do the same for each team and give one point for each correct guess.

Discussion Prompts

1. This game was backwards from regular Charades, with one person guessing instead of one person giving clues. Which way is harder and why?
2. Did your whole team work together or did one person do must of the work?
3. What happened when people worked together versus when they did not?
4. Did it matter who was guessing? Were some people better at it than others?
5. On a team, how important is it to have everyone in a role that is best suited for them?
6. Do you feel you are in the right role on the teams that you are on?

Newscast

Objective
For people to work together to focus on the good qualities in themselves and others.

Group Size
5 or more

Materials
➲ One video camera and one video tape per team

Description
   Break the group into teams of five or six and give each group a video camera and videotape. Have each team use their camera to and create a newscast that everyone is a part of, that features each group member in a story, and that in some way highlights each persons best qualities, talents or skills. After a set time limit gather the groups back together and watch each newscast. You may need to limit the length of the newscasts so there is enough time to watch them all.

Discussion Prompts
1. Was it easier to do a story about others or about yourself?
2. Did people in your group have a wide variety of good qualities?
3. How important is it for teams to be full of people with a variety of talents and skills?
4. Do you feel your talents are used to the fullest as a member of this group?
5. How could you contribute more to the teams that you are on, given your unique talents, skills and attributes?

Variation
➲ Each group makes a newscast about the people of another team and highlights their best qualities.

Together Tasks

Objective
For group members to work together on a variety of tasks.

Group Size
4 or more

Materials
➤ Rope or duct tape

Description
   Gather the group into a clump and tie a rope around them or wrap them in duct tape. Then assign them a variety of tasks to accomplish, such as jumping jacks, running, making a basket, scoring a soccer goal, playing Four Square against other teams, etc. You may simply give one group several tasks as a challenge or have groups compete against each other.

Discussion Prompts
1.   Did this activity make you uncomfortable at all? Why or why not?
2.   Was this an easy challenge for your group?
3.   What was the hardest part of it?
4.   Was communication a factor at all?
5.   How well do you feel your group communicated? What is your evidence of this?

Variation
➤ Have the group line up single file and place their hands on the hips or shoulders of the person in front of them to form a "train" and give them an obstacle course to go through.

Road Map

Objective

For group members to work together to plan an event.

Group Size

4 or more

Materials

- ➲ One map for each team
- ➲ Paper
- ➲ Pens or pencils

Description

Divide the group into teams of two to eight and give each group a map. The map can be of the state you live in, of the whole country, or of a specific area, but give each group a copy of the same map. Instruct the teams to plan a vacation, working within the parameters you set for them. Give each group a list of what they have for their trip, how much money, what kind of car, size of gas tank, m.p.g., price of gas, start or end destination, size of town they can find gas in, amount of time they have, and anything else you think of. Also, give each group paper and a pen or pencil for writing down their travel plans. Any group that runs out of money or gas will be disqualified. You may give "awards" to the team that saw and did the most with what they had, or for the most exhausting trip, the most relaxing, etc.

Discussion Prompts

1. Was this a fun task for your group? Why or why not?
2. Did everyone give the same amount of input?
3. Were any of your ideas rejected? If so, how did you feel? Did you stop giving ideas?
4. What is the hardest part about group decision making?
5. Would you want to go on the trip you planned?
6. Would you want to go on a trip that another group planned?
7. Are vacations usually fun or stressful for you? Why?

Group Clay Creations

Objective
For all group members to contribute to a joint project.

Group Size
4 or more

Materials
- Clay in various colors
- Cardboard pieces or paper plates

Description
   Divide the group into teams of four to eight. (Make sure that there are not more people in each group than you have colors of clay.) Give each group clay in various colors. Each person must take one color of the clay (more than one if there are extra), and this color is the only color that this person can use for the entire activity. Each team must create a sculpture or scene (you may specify the type of scene, such as a town, park, family, etc.) out of the clay, with no sharing of clay with others. For instance, the team decides to make a car, the person with the black clay must make the tires and the person with gray can make some hubcaps, and so on. After each group has made their creation, have them name it and share it with the rest of the group.

Discussion Prompts
1. How did your group decide who got which color?
2. Did some colors have more to do than others?
3. Are you happy with your creation? Why or why not?
4. Would this have been easier for you to do by yourself?
5. Would this have been easier if everyone could use any of the colors? Would everyone have contributed the same amount? Why or why not?
6. Do people usually have an equal part in all group projects?
7. How much do you usually participate in group projects? Why? Is this good or bad?

Lego® Tall Tower

Objective
For each team to work together on a common project.

Group Size
4 or more

Materials
➲ Lego® type building blocks

Description
Prior to the activity, hide Lego® pieces around the room or simply scatter them about. Divide the group into teams of four or more and challenge the groups to build as tall a tower as they can out of the Lego® building blocks. On the "go" signal team members must try to find and gather as many Legos® as they can and then put them together. The winning team is the one with the tallest tower after a given time limit (or after each team has completed the task). Some teams will end up with fewer Legos® than the other teams and will have to be more creative to make their building tall. You may give different awards to each team at the end (i.e., tallest tower with fewest bricks, fastest gatherers, fastest builders, etc.).

Discussion Prompts
1. Was your team very competitive during this game?
2. How did the competition effect the performance of your team? What if there had been no competition and you simply had to build a tall tower out of Legos® you were given?
3. Do you feel competition when on different teams?
4. How do you deal with this competition?

Blind Money

Objective
For group members to learn to trust each other.

Group Size
4 or more

Materials
- 2 quarters for each two people
- A bucket, box or garbage can
- Masking tape

Description
Place a large bucket, box, or garbage can in the center of a circle that has been marked off with tape and have participants get into pairs. Give each pair two quarters and have them stand on the outside of the circle. One person must tip their head back and place one quarter over each of their eyes. Their partner then verbally directs them as they try to walk toward the bucket in the center of the circle and drop their money into it. If they drop their money before getting to the bucket or don't make it into the bucket, they must pick the money up, go back to the edge of the circle, and start over. Do at least two rounds of this game, giving each person the chance to be in both roles.

Discussion Prompts
1. Did you trust your partner? Why or why not?
2. Was it harder to give directions or to receive them? Why?
3. Why are communication and trust both important parts of any partnership?
4. How well do you communicate and how much are you trusted? Are these two elements related?
5. Are you ever "blinded" by money? How?

Video Scavenger Hunt

Objective

For a group of people to work together in a competition.

Group Size

10 or more

Materials

- ➲ One video camera and videotape per team
- ➲ One TV and VCR to watch the tapes on
- ➲ A list of things each group must do (see list that follows)
- ➲ Optional: one vehicle and driver per team

Description

Prior to the activity, create a list of things for the teams to do, and assign a point value for each item (see sample ideas below). Divide the group into teams of four to eight and give each team a video camera, tape, list, and a time to return. You may have cars and drivers for each team, or you may come up with a list of things that can be done in the surrounding area. Each team can use only five minutes of tape and must try to get as many different things in this five minutes as possible. (Or each team only gets to film five thirty-second scenes and tries to fit as many things as possible in each scene.) After the time limit the group must return (deduct points for each minute they are late) and hand over the videotape. Allow time to watch each tape, and tally points as you watch the videos.

Video Scavenger Hunt List Ideas

1. A man with a beard shaking hands with someone on your team – 50 points
2. The whole team singing a song by a stop sign – 100 points
3. Someone on your team getting a drink out of a drinking fountain while someone else is riding piggyback on his/her back – 30 points

4. Someone washing the window of a car of someone they don't know (ask first!) – 50 points
5. The whole team standing in a bathtub while the water is running – 150 points
6. Someone on your team hitting a tennis ball with a tennis racket against a wall that the whole team is standing against – 100 points
7. Someone shaking hands with a policeman – 200 points
8. The whole team in a boat – 150 points
9. The whole team singing a song while in a restaurant - 100 points (50 extra points for each person not on your team that is singing the song as well)
10. Someone on your team walking the dog of someone they don't know – 200 points

Discussion Prompts
1. Did someone in your group emerge as a leader? Was this helpful?
2. Did your group waste a lot of time trying to decide what to do next?
3. How did the team decide where to go and what to do?
4. Are you usually more of a leader or more of a follower? Do you like this trait in yourself?

Hula Walk

Objective
To promote teamwork and cooperation.

Group Size
3 or more

Materials
➲ Several Hula-Hoops

Description
   Line group members up side by side, give them Hula-Hoops and have them connect themselves in the following manner: One person puts his/her right leg inside a Hula-Hoop. The person next to them puts their left leg inside the same hoop, pulling the hoop taut so that it isn't dragging on the ground. That person then puts his/her right leg into another hoop, and so on, until the entire line of people is connected by Hula-Hoops. Those on the ends will have their outside leg free. Once everyone is connected the group must try to walk across a designated area without letting the hoops fall. This can also be done with two rows of people, one in the back and one in the front, all connected using the same hoops. Have smaller groups take turns if there aren't very many hoops.

Discussion Prompts
1. Was this easy or difficult for the group? Why?
2. What obstacles did you encounter while doing this activity?
3. Is it easier for you to overcome obstacles on your own or when with a group? Why?

Variation
➲ Use string or elastic bands instead of hoops.

Snack Auction

Objective
For group members to work together to accomplish tasks and to make decisions quickly.

Group Size
8 or more

Materials
- Play money
- Various snacks

Description
For the first part of this activity, divide the group into teams of four or more and give the teams different challenges to accomplish in a certain amount of time. Assign each challenge a dollar amount, and award any team that successfully accomplishes the task that much money. When the time is up, each team must sit together as a group with all their money..

For the second part of this activity, set up a table at the front of the room. Under the table, out of view of the participants, have a box of snacks (bags of chips, cupcakes, carrots, soda, cups, etc.). Place one item on the table at a time, allowing the team to bid or not bid on the item, auction style. Give each item to the highest bidder, and don't let them know how many snacks you sill have left. Teams will have to decide if they want to use all their money early or chance it and wait for a better snack later (that might not come). At the end of the auction have a snack picnic!

Discussion Prompts
1. Did you agree on everything your team did today?
2. How did your team make decisions? Was everyone involved?
3. How do you make decisions quickly when on a team? Is it possible?
4. How do you feel about the snacks your team ended up with?

Object Skit

Objective
For group members to work together to solve problems.

Group Size
8 or more

Materials
➲ Various odd objects

Description
   Divide the group into teams of four or more and give each team an object. The object can be anything, a kitchen tool, an office supply, toy, etc. You may give each team the same object or have them each select a different object from an assortment that you provide. Give the groups about ten minutes to plan a skit that utilizes the object as a prop in as many ways as possible. Allow time for each group to perform their skit, and give a point for each purposeful use of the object as a prop the group comes up with.

Discussion Prompt
1. How did your group decide on what to do for your skit? Was everyone involved in the planning process?
2. Do you feel your group was creative? Why or why not?
3. Is it harder or easier to be creative as a group versus by yourself? Why?
4. What is the hardest part about being creative as a group versus being creative by yourself? What is the easiest part?
5. How can a group enhance the creative process? Do you utilize this as a member of a group? Why or why not?

Talk-Through Target Practice

Objective

For one group member to receive feedback and directions from others in order to be successful.

Group Size

2 or more

Materials

- ➲ Beanbags or small balls
- ➲ Boxes or buckets
- ➲ Blindfolds

Description

Divide the group into teams of two or more. Give each team a blindfold and a pile of beanbags or small balls (or have one pile and groups take turns). Set up one or more buckets or boxes to be used as targets and make a line on the floor for people to throw from. Each team selects one person to be the blindfolded thrower, who stands behind the line and is given one beanbag at a time. He/she must try to toss the beanbag into the target, getting a point for each successful toss. The tosser's teammates give him/her feedback after each throw (too far, too soft, too low, etc.) to help guide the next throw. If time permits, play enough rounds for everyone to get to play both roles.

Discussion Prompts

1. Was it easier to be the thrower or the direction giver? Why?
2. Was patience a factor at all during this activity? How well did you do with this?
3. How do you feel your team communicated during this activity?
4. Did the verbal directions help or could you have done just as well without them?
5. Do you ever rely on directions from others? Why or why not?

This Is Your Group

Objective
For team members to work together both creatively and responsively.

Group Size
6 or more

Materials
➲ Paper
➲ Pens or pencils

Description
Divide the group into two or more teams of three or more and give each team paper and a pen or pencil. Assign each group to another team. Have them write down all of the names of the people in that group and then write a story about them. When all the stories are finished, gather the groups back together. Ask one person from each team to read their story, while the people the story is about act it out. Repeat for each team.

Discussion Prompts
1. What did you think of the story that was written about you?
2. In what aspect of this activity did your team have to work together the most, the story writing or the skit? Why?
3. Which kind of teamwork is most difficult, physical or decision-making? Why?

Variation
➲ Each story must affirm each participant by highlighting their good qualities.

Seesaw

Objective
For partners to coordinate their efforts toward a common goal.

Group Size
2 or more

Materials
- 2x6 board (at least 6 feet long) for each pair (or take turns)
- A block of wood or cement about 4" high and 4" to 6" wide for each pair (or take turns)

Description
This game is a balancing challenge. First, place the center of the board on the block of wood or cement. Have one person stand at each end of the seesaw, inching forward until the seesaw is perfectly balanced. Both participants must continue to move towards the middle of the board until their inside feet touch. The challenge is to do this without the board touching the ground from the time it is balanced till the time the two people meet in the middle. To make this challenge more difficult, make each pair start over each time their board touches the ground.

Discussion Prompts
1. How did you and your partner approach this problem?
2. Was this frustrating for anyone? Why or why not?
3. Did some pairs have an advantage over others?
4. What factors made this activity easy or hard?
5. Do you sometimes feel the teams you are on are at a disadvantage? If so, how do you overcome this?

Variations

➲ You may have more than one pair going at a time on separate boards and make it a competition to see which team can balance and meet in the middle first.

➲ You may use a wider board to make it easier to stand on.

➲ Create a story about how the team must cross a canyon to a middle point and this board is the only way to safety. Have the teams come up with a way to use the board as a seesaw.

Pipeline

Objective

For group members to work together to decide how to solve a problem and then to implement the solution.

Group Size

6 to 12 (or break a larger group into teams)

Materials

- Construction paper (at least one per person)
- ½ sheet of white paper, crumpled into a tight ball and taped securely
- Tape
- Scissors
- Various other materials

Description

Give the group the paper ball, a stack of construction paper, roll of tape, and various other objects (these are simply to add to the challenge but not needed to solve the problem).

Then set up an area that is at least twice as many feet across as there are group members. Instruct the group to get the ball across this area while abiding by the following rules:

1. The ball must roll to the other side
2. The ball may not touch the ground at any time
3. No one may touch the ball at any time once in enters the area
4. Each person must be involved in the process of moving the ball
5. If any of these rules are broken the group must start over.

There may be other solutions, here is one possibility. Each person rolls up one piece of paper into a tube. Standing side by side, team members hold their pipes in front of them, connecting all the pipes to make a long tube through which to roll the ball. As soon as the ball goes through one tube, that person runs to the other end of the line to lengthen the pipe. Each person does this until the pipeline reaches the other side and the ball makes it across!

Discussion Prompts

1. How did you feel about this task when you heard all of the rules?
2. What process did your team go through when solving this?
3. Did the problem-solving or the physical challenge prove to be more difficult for your group? Why
4. What type of situation do you find to be most difficult to deal with when working as a part of a team?

Water Over the Bridge

Objective
To practice problem solving.

Group Size
4 or more

Materials
- A stack of 3x5 index cards
- Tape
- Scissors
- String
- Blue Construction Paper
- Large plastic cups
- Water
- Optional: tin foil, paper towel rolls, straws, etc.

Description
Divide the group into teams of at least four people each. Give each team a piece of blue construction paper that is at least four inches wide, a stack of 3x5 cards, scissors, tape, string, and anything else you have gathered.

Tell the group that the blue paper is the river and their job is to make a bridge over the river out of the materials given to them. The bridge cannot touch the river, it must be at least four inches tall (to withstand the floods), and it must be strong enough to hold eight ounces of water in a paper cup without any of the water spilling.

Discussion Prompts

1. What process did your group go through when building your bridge?
2. How did your group come to an agreement?
3. How did your group handle disagreements?
4. What was the hardest part of this activity for your group?
5. What did you learn about yourself from doing this activity?
6. What did you learn about your team as a result of doing this activity?

Through The Hoop

Objective
For group members to work together to accomplish a common goal.

Group Size
6 or more

Materials
➲ Four pieces of rope
➲ Hula-Hoop

Description
   For this activity you need to find two trees or posts. Tie the Hula-Hoop vertically between the two trees. Start by putting it just a few feet off of the ground. Challenge the group to get everyone through it without anyone touching any part of the hoop. After the team has done this, raise the hoop and challenge them to do the same thing. See how high the group can get the hoop and still get everyone through it.

Discussion Prompts
1. Did different people have different roles in this activity? What role did you take?
2. Do you feel you gave the group an advantage or a disadvantage? How did this make you feel?
3. In what types of teamwork activities do you have more of an advantage and support your team the most?

Variation
➲ Do this as a competition to see which team can get everyone through at the highest level or put the hoop at a certain height and see which team can get the most people through.

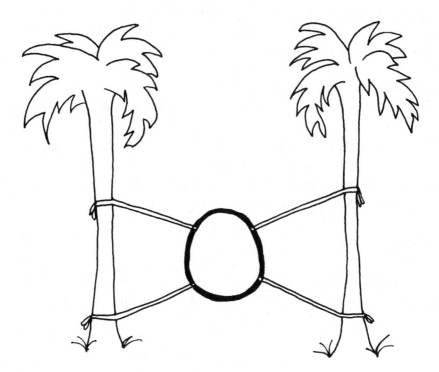

Team Up

Pencil Drop

Objective
For two people to work together as partners to complete a physical challenge.

Group Size
2 or more

Materials
- String
- Pencil
- Bottle

Description
Before starting the game, tie two pieces of string around the eraser end of a pencil. Choose two players, and have them stand back to back. Tie the ends of the string around their waists so that the pencil is hanging down between them. Now place an empty bottle between the two and challenge them to lower the pencil into the bottle without using their hands. You can have different groups doing this at the same time as a race, or time several pairs to see who does it the fastest, or simply use it as a fun challenge.

Discussion Prompts
1. How do you feel you and your partner did?
2. What factors made this difficult for you and your partner?
3. What factors made this easy for you and your partner?

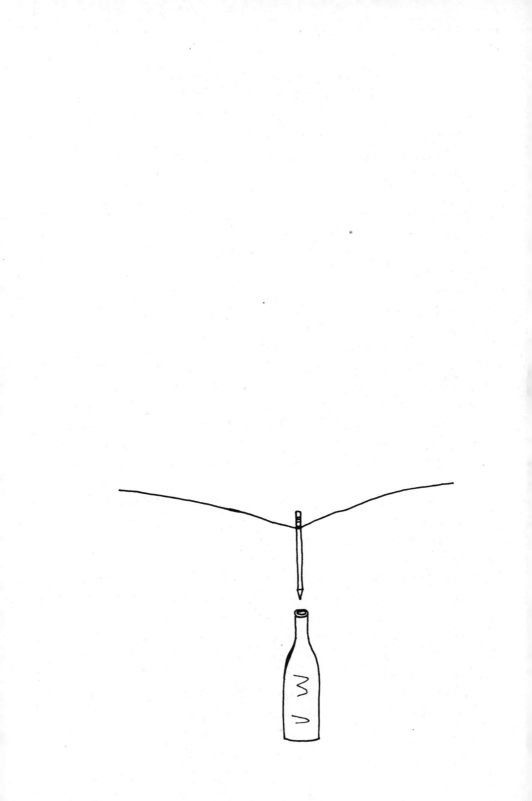

Bridge Toss

Objective

For group members to work together to solve what appears to be an individual problem.

Group Size

6 to 12 is ideal

Materials

➲ 1 Frisbee® (or similar object) per person

Description

Mark off an area that the group must get across and give each person a Frisbee®. Challenge the group to use their Frisbees® to make a bridge across the area while abiding by the following rules:

1. No one can touch the ground inside the area with any part of their body.
2. Each person gets one chance to throw their Frisbee® into the area from the same starting line. Once it lands on the ground and stops it cannot be moved (although it may be turned upside down so it doesn't break when people walk on it).
3. You may not enter the area until after you throw your Frisbee®.
4. You may only cross to the other side by stepping on the Frisbees®
5. Once all of the Frisbees have been thrown, if your group cannot make it across you must start over.

Tell the group only the rules above and let them take the challenge. Some groups may be able to throw the Frisbees® perfectly and make a bridge (this is easier done on grass than on a surface that allows the Frisbees® to skid). Or, they may throw them one at a time, walk to the end of the bridge and have the next person pass their Frisbee® down the line until it can be placed on the ground.

TIP: You may want to omit rule number three in order to make it more challenging for the group to figure out the answer.

Discussion Prompts

1. How did you account for different Frisbee®-throwing skills in the group?
2. Was the answer to this problem obvious at first?
3. If someone came up with an answer, did everyone else see the same answer before this person said it?
4. Some things are obvious once we see them, but not at first. How do we find the answers to things that aren't obvious? How does being a part of a team help with this?

Twinkie® Tower

Objective
For people to work together to solve a problem in a way that gives the team the maximum reward at the end.

Group Size
2 or more

Materials
- 1 box of wrapped Twinkies® per team
- 1 box of mixed plastic silverware per team
- 1 3x5 index card per team

Description
This activity can be done with one or more teams depending on the group size. Teams should have two to eight players each. Give each team one box of individually wrapped Twinkies® (they usually come in a box of ten), one small box or bag of plastic silverware, and one 3x5 index card.

Then give the following challenge: Use the Twinkies® and the silverware to create a structure that is at least 3" tall. The 3x5 card is to be used only as a measuring device. Any Twinkies not used in the structure itself can be placed on the structure. At the end of a given time limit, any Twinkies® supported by the structure and still in their wrapper may be eaten. Any Twinkies® that are not supported on the structure or that were used in the building of the structure may not be eaten.

Discussion Prompts

1. Were you happy with your reward at the end?
2. How did you decide the number of Twinkies® used in the structure?
3. Did everyone on your team agree with all of the decisions being made?
4. Did everyone on your team strive to save as many Twinkies® as possible?
5. How do you feel your team did during this challenge? What is your proof?

Variation

➲ This can be done with other wrapped food items that people would like to eat at the end of the game.

Team Choice

Objective
For team members to all agree on a decision even when everyone doesn't share the same opinions.

Group Size
2 or more

Materials
➲ None

Description
Make a list of things that people must choose between (some ideas follow). Divide the group into smaller teams if you have a large group and give the teams different choices. To make this activity more effective you should have two sides of the room for them to go to that represent their answer. You might say, "If your team chooses 'A' go to this side of the room or if your team chooses 'B' go to that side of the room." After each choice, have team members explain why they chose what they did. You can make the choices as personal or as light as you feel is appropriate for your group. Below are some choice ideas that range from light to personal.

Choice Ideas
1. For a vacation, would your team rather go to:
   A. Beach Resort or B. Ski Resort
2. For Christmas, would your team rather get:
   A. New bike or B. Canoe
3. Would your team rather have lunch with:
   A. The President or B. A movie star of your choice
4. On Sunday would your team rather go to:
   A. Church or B. Football game
5. Would your team rather vote:
   A. Republican or B. Democrat
6. Would your team rather have:
   A. More money or B. More vacation time

Discussion Prompts

1. How did you feel if your team went against your preference? Did you go with them anyway? Why or why not?
2. When part of a team, do you always agree with the decisions made?
3. What do you do when you don't agree with the decision made by your team?
4. How can teammates compromise when they don't all agree?

Four Corners Crossing

Objective
For teammates to work together with each other as well as with members of other teams.

Group Size
12 to 24 is ideal

Materials
➲ Paper plates, paper, carpet squares, small boards or card board, or a mixture of these or other items that can be placed on the ground and stepped on by one or two people at time

Description
For this activity you need a large open area. Place the paper plates (or whatever items you have available) in the pattern shown in the diagram. There should be two diagonal paths running from corner to corner and crossing in the middle. The lines do not need to be straight but may curve and twist. They should, however, be roughly the same.

Divide the group into four teams and assign one team to each corner. Give them the following rules:

1. You must travel from your corner to the opposite corner.
2. You may not touch the ground and may only travel by stepping on the spots (plates, etc.)
3. If you touch the ground, you must go back to your original corner and start over.
4. A spot becomes activated once someone steps on it. As long as someone is touching it, it will stay in activation and can be used.
5. Once an activated spot becomes deactivated (no one is touching it after the initial touch), it floats away (leader removes it) and it can no longer be used for the remainder of the activity.
6. Your team is successful when all members of <u>all four teams</u> are standing in the corner opposite the one they started from.
7. Spots cannot be picked up and moved.

The best solution is for each team to travel on one path to the middle, then share the spots in the middle, keeping at least one person on the middle spots until everyone has a chance to cross over.

Discussion Prompts
1. Did your team work with the other teams or did you just make your own plan?
2. Did you have to think about others during this process?
3. Are you ever competitive with other teams when you should be working with them?
4. When you are working as a part of a team, do you ever need help from other teams?
5. How do you communicate to another team what your needs and what you have to offer to them?

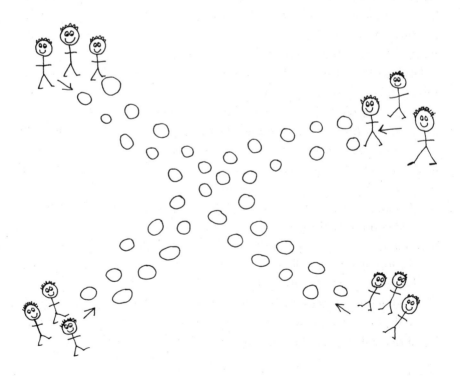

Heel Walk

Objective
For everyone to contribute to a group effort.

Group Size
3 or more

Materials
➲ None

Description
Make sure everyone is wearing shoes for this activity! Have the group line up single file with their heels on the toes of the person behind them. The group must then attempt to walk as a unit without becoming disconnected. You may give them a certain distance to walk or ask them to set a goal as to how far they can walk as a group. For an added challenge, place obstacles in the area for the group to walk around.

Discussion Prompts
1. Do you think this would have been easier for you if you were in a different place in line? Why or why not?
2. How was communication a factor in this activity?
3. How big a line do you think could be made?

Variation
➲ Start with pairs, then have each pair join another pair. Keep making the groups bigger until everyone is in the line together.

Knot Race

Objective
For people to work together to set and reach a goal.

Group Size
8 or more is ideal

Materials
- A long rope or piece of webbing
- A stopwatch

Description
Take a long rope or piece of webbing and tie the ends together securely to create a large circle. Gather the group into a circle and have each person hold onto the rope with both hands. Pass the knot around the circle by having group members slide their hands along the rope. Have each person share something about themselves as the knot comes to them.

Once the knot has gone all the way around the circle and back to the you, ask the group how fast they think they can pass the knot completely around the circle. Have the group decide on a time and announce it to you. The group then attempts to pass the knot around as fast as they can while you time it. After the first round, announce their time and challenge them to beat it. Do several rounds of this until the group beats its own goal or is satisfied with the speed they have achieved.

Discussion Prompts
1. Was it easy or difficult to decide on a time estimate? How did the group finally decide on a time? Did this involve any teamwork?
2. How did you feel after the first round?
3. Did you want to adjust your goal time at any point? Why or why not?
4. How did your team work together to beat your own time?
5. Are you often competitive against yourself? Why or why not? Is this good or bad?

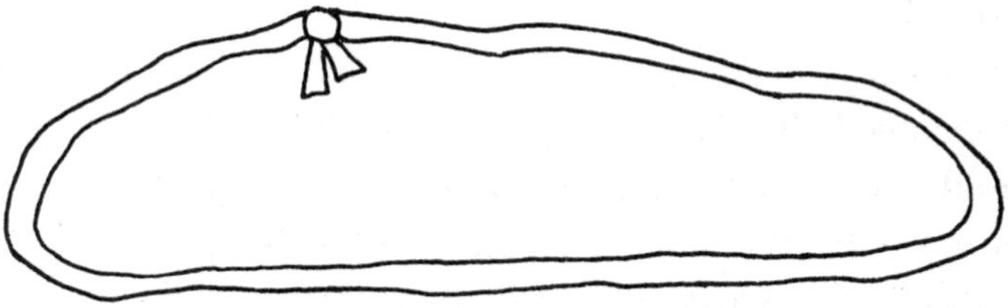

Low Electric Fence

Objective
For people to work together as a team.

Group Size
6 to 15 is ideal

Materials
➲ Rope or bungee cord
➲ Two sturdy trees or poles (optional)

Description
Tie a piece of rope or bungee between two sturdy trees or poles, or have two people hold the rope. It should be at about the height of the inseam of the average person in the group so that it is a bit difficult to step over the rope without touching it, but not much higher.

Have all of the group members stand on one side of the "fence" and challenge them to get everyone on the team over it without touching it. For the duration of this activity, everyone must be touching at least one other person in the group, and the whole group must be connected. Contact spots may be changed as long as contact with the group is never lost. If anyone touches the fence or looses contact with the group, the whole group must start over. Alternatively, you can give that person a blindfold for the rest of the activity.

For safety, it is important that you have spotters for this activity who are ready to help steady someone who is about to fall when climbing over the fence.

Discussion Prompts
1. How did the group come up with a plan?
2. Was safety a factor during this activity?
3. Do you often watch out for the safety of the others in the group?
4. Do you feel that others watch out for your safety?
5. What are some ways you can watch out for each other in other situations?

Stuck Together

Objective
For group members to show patience when working together on a task that can be frustrating and time consuming.

Group Size
4 to 20 is ideal

Materials
- One role of masking tape
- Rope, tarp, or blanket (optional)

Description
Give the group a boundary that they must all stand in or on such as the key on a basketball court, an old blanket or tarp, or an area marked off with rope. Once the entire group is in the designated area give them one new roll of masking tape. Challenge the group to stay in this area and to unroll the entire roll of tape while attaching it to the group members. They must not tear the tape, and they cannot let the tape touch itself. Also, the tape can only touch skin and not clothing. If the tape breaks it may be stuck back together at that spot. The tape must touch each member of the group and be entirely unrolled. Once the entire group is "stuck together," ask them to walk as a unit to the next activity or to another area without breaking the tape.

Discussion Prompts
1. Was this a frustrating activity for anyone? Why or why not?
2. How did the group come up with a plan? Or did one person come up with a plan?
3. How did you decide who got to hold the tape first?
4. Do you feel this group has lots of patience? Is this helpful to the group?
5. What was the most challenging part of this activity for the group? For you?

People Pull

Objective
For group members to ask one another for help when trying to accomplish a difficult task.

Group Size
10 to 15 is ideal (or break a larger group into smaller teams)

Materials
➲ None

Description
At the beginning of the activity ask for the biggest, strongest person to volunteer (or have the team select this person). The person selected must lie down on the ground, stiff, with arms to the side. Now choose one of the smaller people in the group to try to pull this person up to a standing position using only one hand. When they fail, tell them that they can ask one person to help them, but this person can only use one hand as well. If they still can't do it, allow the new person to select another person to help. Continue in this manner until the person on the ground is successfully lifted. It is possible that not everyone will be chosen to help lift the person but this can lead to good discussion about each person having different abilities and how in other situations they would be the first person chosen to help.

For safety, it is important that you have spotters for this activity to make sure that the person being lifted is not dropped.

Discussion Prompts
1. Why is it important to ask for help sometimes?
2. Is it always easy to ask others for help?
3. If you weren't chosen to help or if you were one of the last ones chosen, why do you think this is?

4. Can you think of another situation in which you would be the first person who was asked for help? What is it and why?
5. In what ways do individuals all contribute to a final outcome that cannot be accomplished by a single person on this team?

Magic Boots

Objective
For the group to use problem solving skills in order to accomplish a difficult task.

Group Size
5 to 15 is ideal

Materials
➲ Boundary markers

Description
   Mark off an area that the group must get across that is at least ten feet long (longer for an added challenge) Tell the group that the ground is made of quicksand (or any other substance that they do no want to step in) and that the only way to get across is to wear a pair of magic boots. Only one person may be walking in the quicksand at a time since there is only one pair of magic boots. Each person may only walk across the area once because the magic boots only work once for each person. The magic boots must be handed off from one person to the next in the following manner: The wearer places their hands on the feet of another person and says, "I give you the magic boots" (or make up some other fun slogan). Team members are allowed to carry one another (in fact, some will have to be carried), and the magic boots may be used to cross in either direction.
   This activity takes some planning!

Discussion Prompts

1. Did this seem easy or impossible when the task was first given to you?
2. How did your team come up with a plan?
3. Did some people have an easier job than others?
4. Do people usually have different skills and talents to offer to your team?
5. How does the diversity of your team add to your effectiveness?

Rope Knots

Objective

For each person to contribute to the overall success of the group by doing his/her individual part and by helping others when they need it.

Group Size

8 to 20 is ideal

Materials

➲ One long climbing rope

Description

This is a fun variation to the popular game Knots, where people grab each other's hands and try to get untangled. In this game there is less human contact, so it is less threatening but still a challenge.

Tie one overhand knot in the rope for each person that is in the group. Space the knots about two feet apart. Instruct group members to select a knot on the rope and stand by it on either side of the rope. Then tell them to grab the rope on either side of the knot with one hand. Some people will grab further out from their knot than others, but that is OK. Now challenge the group to untie all of the knots without anyone letting go of the rope or without moving the hand that is on the rope. Participants may use only their free hand to untie knots.

You may set this activity up by having the group think of things that are "knots" for the group that need to be "untied," or have the knots represent problems for the group that need to be straightened out.

Discussion Prompts

1. How many different groups were working on this challenge at once?
2. When your side of the rope was untied, did you help the others on your team in any way, or did you just hang out? Why?
3. Are you ever on a team where two or more different groups are working separate of each other?
4. Is this a positive thing for the team?
5. Are there any "knots" on your team that need to be untangled?

Mountain Top

Objective
For group members to work together for the good of the group.

Group Size
8 to 15 is ideal

Materials
- A rope hanging from the ceiling (i.e., gym climbing rope)
- Rope or other boundary marker
- 2 coffee cans or similar height blocks or cans
- 1 pole, stick, or piece of pipe about 1" in diameter

Description
Set up the two coffee cans with a pole set horizontally across them about three or four feet to one side of the rope. On the other side of the rope, use a different piece of rope to make a circle that the whole group can stand in. For added challenge make the circle small so the group must work together to stand in it without falling out of the boundary. This circle should be about three to four feet from the rope as well.

Set this activity up by telling a story that requires the group to get from a cliff to the mountaintop some distance away. Starting behind the "cliff" (pole) they must get hold of the climbing rope without stepping off the "cliff". Once they have the rope, they must swing across to the other side and land on the "mountain" (the rope circle). Only one person may go across at once at a time. If anyone steps out of the boundary, knocks the pole off of the cans, or touches the ground, the group must start over. For safety reasons, the leader should stand near the climbing rope to catch anyone who falls.

Discussion Prompts

1. How did the group come up with a plan?
2. How did the order that you went in factor in to the plan?
3. How did you ensure that your teammates were safe during this activity?
4. How would this activity have been different if there was a real cliff and a real mountaintop?
5. Would you trust your teammates if it were real? Why or why not?
6. How can you build trust as a team?

Variations

➔ Give group members things to carry with them to the mountain for an added challenge.
➔ Set up a low platform for the group to stand on in place of the circle.

Ball Ring

Objective

For group members to work together on a frustrating challenge without cheating.

Group Size

6 to 12 is ideal

Materials

- A round key chain type of ring big enough to set a golf ball on
- 12 pieces of string 4 to 5 feet long
- 1 golf ball
- 2 paper cups
- 1 long rope

Description

Prior to the activity, tie the ends of the strings to the ring. Place the ring on top of an upside-down paper cup with the twelve strings going out in all directions, and place a golf ball on the ring. Place the rope in a circle around the cup just beyond the ends of the strings.

To begin the activity, have each person grab the end of one string (some may need to have more than one). Place a second paper cup some distance away (or at the next activity that you will be going to) and challenge the group to pick up the ball with the ring and carry it to the other cup. Nobody can go inside the rope circle at any time. Also, once the ball leaves the circle, no one can talk until the ball is successfully placed on the other cup. If the ball falls to the ground, the group must start over.

Discussion Prompts

1. Was this frustrating for anyone?
2. How do you feel about starting over when something doesn't go right?
3. How did each individual affect the rest of the team?
4. Was it easier or more difficult to work as a team when you couldn't talk? Why?
5. How can you communicate to your teammates other than talking? How can this be helpful to the team?

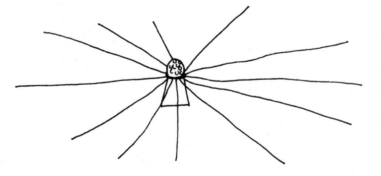

Balloon Tower

Objective
For group members to work together with everyone contributing to the project.

Group Size
3 or more

Materials
- 30 balloons per team
- 1 roll of tape per team

Description
Divide the group into teams of three to eight. Give each group a pile of thirty balloons that are not blown up and a roll of tape. Challenge the groups to make the tallest tower they can out of the balloons and tape. You may give the group a time limit for this activity, or you may challenge them to build a tower that is at least as tall as the smallest group member.

Discussion Prompts
1. How did your plan change as you began to build?
2. Did everyone agree with the building plan?
3. How did you handle it if you didn't agree? Did everyone vocalize their feelings? Why or why not?
4. How did you feel when a balloon popped? Why?
5. How do you feel about your finished tower?
6. What do you think you should name your tower based on how you group did?

Variation
- Give the group time to plan the activity before they are allowed to start and then do not allow them to talk once they start building.

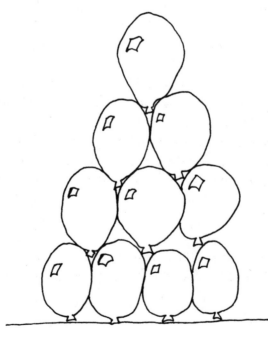

Team Up

Horizontal Spider's Web

Objective
To solve a problem as a group and to help each other when implementing the solution.

Group Size
6 to 12

Materials
- Bungee chord, rope, string, or masking tape
- 2 tables

Description
This activity is a variation of the popular Spider's Web challenge, where group members go through a series of holes to get to the other side. In this version the web is placed horizontally between two tables with at least one hole in the web per person in the group (it's nice to have a couple of extra holes). The web is made by taping string horizontally between the two tables so that holes are formed. Make the holes different sizes. The smallest person in the group should be able to fit through the smallest hole without touching the sides of the web.

Challenge the group to get each member through one of the holes without anyone touching the web at all. Once a person goes through one hole it becomes closed off and no one else may pass through that hole. Each person must pass through the top and out the bottom of the web. Once someone is standing in their hole they can help others get to more difficult holes in the middle, but you may or may not want to give them this hint.

Discussion Prompts

1. Did each person contribute something different to the group or did everyone contribute equally? How did this affect the group?
2. What did you individually contribute to the team today?
3. Was this an easy challenge for you or difficult?
4. If it was easy, how did you help others?
5. If it was difficult, how did others help you?
6. Do you like to ask for help when on a team? Why or why not?
7. How can helping each other improve a team's performance? Does this team help each other as much as it should? Do people ask for help as much as they should?

Black Hole

Objective
For the entire group to participate in a challenge.

Group Size
6 or more

Materials
➲ A bungee cord

Description
Prior to the activity get a piece of thin bungee chord and securely tie it into a loop that is at least one foot in diameter when not stretched out (make it larger if you have larger sized members in your group).

Present the loop to the group and tell them that it is a black hole that will let you travel through time (and make up a good story about where the group will be going and why). At this point do not reveal to the group the fact that the hole is made of bungee cord and can be stretched. Ask them if they think the whole group can get through the hole.

At this point give the group the following rules:

1. No more than two people may touch the hole at a time.
2. Once you start, at least one person has to have contact with the hole at all times.
3. Once a person touches the hole and lets go, they may not touch it again.
4. You may not touch the hole at all when passing through it.

Also, based on how large the group is decide on how many people can go through the hole the same way. For instance, for a group of about fifteen, tell them that no more than four people can go through the hole in the same manner. Give the group one minute to come up with a plan before allowing them to touch the hole.

Discussion Prompts

1. Did you think you could fit through the hole when the problem was first presented to you?

2. How did you view the problem once it was discovered that the hole could stretch?

3. Do you ever think a problem is more difficult to solve than it really is and feel frustrated before getting all of the information?

Variation

⮑ Have the group stay connected with at least one other group member when they pass through the hole.

Sheet Scoop

Objective
For group members to work together on a project.

Group Size
4 or more

Materials
- One bed sheet for every 4 to 6 people

Description
Give each group of four to six people one old bed sheet and designate a gathering spot for each team. Instruct the groups to use their sheet to gather as many objects as they can within a given time period and to bring these objects back to their designated spot. At no time can anyone touch any part of any of the objects with any part of his/her body. Only the sheets can be used for lifting and carrying the objects.

You may challenge the groups to gather the most objects or to create the biggest pile or to get the biggest object (base this on the area you are doing the activity in).

Discussion Prompts
1. Did everyone on your team go in the same direction at all times?
2. Did your team work with each other, or did you sometimes work against each other?
3. How did your group make decisions? Were you a part of the decision making, or did you let others lead?
4. Who was the leader of your group? Why?
5. Do you tend to be more of a leader or follower? Why? Would you like to change this about yourself? If so, how can you do this?

Garbage Collector

Objective
For people to practice communication skills when a part of a team.

Group Size
3 or more

Materials
- 1 garbage-type bag for each group of three to four people
- Blindfolds
- Various small objects

Description
Scatter balls, toys, crumpled-up paper, or other items around on the floor. Divide the group into teams of three to four and give each team a plastic garbage bag and a blindfold. Each team must select one person to be blindfolded and carry the garbage bag. The person carrying the bag cannot see the "garbage" but must go around and pick up as much as possible and put it into his/her bag. The teammates of the blindfolded person must verbally direct this person to the garbage pieces, but cannot touch the person or any of the garbage at any time. After all of the items are collected, tell the teams to stop. You may repeat this activity by dumping the items out and scattering them again so each person gets a chance to be the garbage collector.

Discussion Prompts
1. Was it easier to be blindfolded or to give directions? Why?
2. Are you better at giving orders or taking them? Why?
3. Do you ever rely on others for directions or do you always rely on yourself? Does this hurt or help your team?

Variations

⮕ Do this after an activity that has some cleanup involved and have people actually pick up the items that need to be put away, or thrown away.

⮕ Place a garbage can in the area for the blindfolded person to place all of the scattered garbage in. There can be several teams putting garbage into the same can at the same time for an added challenge.

Group Wheelbarrow

Objective
For group members to help one another to accomplish a physical challenge.

Group Size
5 to 20 is ideal

Materials
➲ 2"x4" board at least 6 feet long

Description
   Challenge the group to "do the wheelbarrow" with as many people as possible participating at the same time. (The wheelbarrow is a classic relay race where one person holds anther person's legs up while that person "walks" on their hands.) The group may use the board to support the feet of as many team members as possible while at least two people support the board. Those who are doing the wheelbarrow may be faced either way, but the group as a whole must be able to move at least five feet in one direction (or to a specified destination).

Discussion Prompts
1.   Was it harder to get set up or to travel across the area? Why?
2.   Which job was harder, supporting the group or being a wheelbarrow?
3.   Does you team ever depend on a few people to carry you? Is this good or bad and why?

Variation
➲ For a larger group, you may give them a destination that they must get to wheelbarrow-style and tell them they can only take a certain amount of trips to get everyone across.

Team Up

Up and Over

Objective

For group members to work together to solve a physical problem and to then help each other implement the various solutions.

Group Size

4 or more

Materials

- One 2"x6" board at least 6 feet long
- Boundary markers, or two ropes to make a boundary with

Description

Mark off an area about three feet wide and at least ten feet long. Give the group the board and tell them that each person must travel up and over the area, from one end to the other, without anyone touching the ground or any people. The group may use the board to transport people across the area and may walk alongside of the area but cannot go into the area. You will need spotters for this activity who walk along behind and in front of the person who is being transported to ensure their safety.

For an added challenge tell the group that no more than four people (or any number you choose) can go across in the same manner. Some people may be sitting on the board frontwards, others backwards, some may hang from the board by their hands, etc.

Discussion Prompts

1. How did you decide who was going to carry your team?
2. Do some people in your group have different strengths than others? How can these be used to support the group?
3. What strengths do you have that support the group?

Team Up

Buddy Blind Draw

Objective

For group members to practice communication and teamwork.

Group Size

3 or more

Materials

- Large sheets of paper (or chalkboard or whiteboard) and writing implements
- Blindfolds

Description

Divide the group into teams of three and give each team two blindfolds and two writing implements. Have each team select two of its members to be blindfolded. The third member will go to the leader, who names an object that the blindfolded teammates must draw. This person goes back to his or her teammates and, standing between them, links arms with them. He or she then instructs the teammates how to draw the object without telling them what the object is. Each blindfolded person uses their outside hand to draw as their leader tries to coordinate their efforts.

Discussion Prompts

1. Did you accomplish the task given to you?
2. Was anyone frustrated? Why or why not?
3. Did you understand clearly the directions that were given to you if you were one of the people who was drawing?
4. How did you support each other during this activity?
5. How can you support your teammates in any situation that comes up?

Variation

➲ If you have several teams playing give each team a different object to
   draw and have other teams try to guess what it is that the group drew.

Disc Walk

Objective
For a group of people to work together to solve a physical problem.

Group Size
2 to 6 is ideal

Materials
- ⊃ 1 Frisbee®-type flying disc for each 2 to 6 participants
- ⊃ Optional: Various items to be used as obstacles, (balls, etc.)

Description
Place a Frisbee® upside down on the ground and . Have two to six people stand around the disc. Placing one finger each inside the lip of the disc, and the group should lift the disc into the air without dropping it. Once the disc is up, give the group another task to do while holding it: walk a certain distance, go through obstacles, or pass a soccer ball to each other with their feet without dropping the disc, etc.

Discussion Prompts
1. What was the most difficult aspect of this challenge?
2. How did your team deal with the disc dropping or falling?
3. How do you feel about starting over when your team fails?
4. Do you ever approach the problem differently the second time or do you always keep doing it the same way? Is this positive or negative for your team?

Team Build

Objective
For each person to add to the final success of the various team projects.

Group Size
4 or more

Materials
- Lego®-type building blocks with instructions and/or pictures on how to build specific projects
- Small plastic zipper bags

Description
Prior to the activity, create kits for Lego® projects with the blocks. Distribute the pieces into bags, one for each person — but do not put all the pieces for each kit into the same bag. Post the instructions and/or pictures around the room.

Give each person a bag of Lego® pieces. Challenge them to figure out which sculpture they go with and build the projects. They will need to cooperate with each other!

Discussion Prompts
1. Did anyone take a leadership role during this activity?
2. Was teamwork involved in this activity?
3. How did you contribute to the team?
4. In what ways was communication a factor during this activity?
5. When is communication a key factor for your team?

Give Me My Shoes!

Objective
For individuals to give clear directions to members of their team who must use good listening skills in order to successfully accomplish a task.

Group Size
8 to 20 is ideal

Materials
- 2 blindfolds

Description
Have the entire group place their shoes into a large pile and divide the group into two teams, A and B. Ask each team to select one person to be blindfolded. The rest of the participants should make a circle around the shoe pile, standing in AB order.

On the "go" signal the two people who are blindfolded must try to find the shoes of each person on his/her own team and hand them to the correct person. Only verbal directions can be given, with no touching or guiding allowed. Those in the circle should stay in the same place throughout the activity.

Discussion Prompts
1. Was there any confusion during this activity?
2. How did your team deal with the confusion?
3. If you were blindfolded, how did you know which voices to listen to?
4. Do you ever have lots of different voices telling you what to do at the same time?
5. How do you decide which is the best voice to listen to?
6. Do you always choose the best voice? Why or why not?

Variation
- Have more than two teams going at once to make the game go faster.

Team Up

Party Theme

Objective
For small teams of people to work together for the good of the whole group.

Group Size
4 or more

Materials
- Various decorating supplies (i.e., colored paper, crepe paper, tissue paper, ink pens, scissors, tape, etc.)
- Optional: Snacks

Description
You will need to have a few separate rooms for this activity or be able to divide one room into different sections. Divide the group into teams (base the amount of teams on how many rooms you have). Give each team a box of supplies that can be used to decorate a room. Give them a theme for their room or have each team select their own. Set a time limit, and have them decorate their room for a party that matches their theme. They must also plan at least one activity to do while at their party. You may also provide different snacks for each group to serve.

Once each group has finished getting their room and activity ready, have a group party with each team leading their own part of the party in their own room. Have fun!

Discussion Prompts
1. How did your team come to an agreement on how to decorate your room?
2. Did you feel any pressure to make your room really nice since others would be seeing it?
3. Did you compare your room to the other rooms? Why or why not?
4. How successful do you think our party was today? Why?

Junkyard Crossing

Objective
For group members to work together toward a goal.

Group Size
8 to 12 is ideal

Materials
➲ Various items that can be used to stand on and that can be moved

Description
Set up a "junkyard" that the group must get across without getting "bitten" by the junkyard dog. Designate a line on the ground as the start point and do the same for an end point about ten yards away. Create a story about the junkyard and challenge the group to cross it without anyone touching the ground inside the junkyard, because the dog will charge you if you are on the ground (or something like that).

Provide the group with various items for them to use when crossing the junkyard that people can stand on and that can be picked up and moved. Some good items are: an old tire, a chunk of wood, a piece of a tarp or blanket, a flattened cardboard box, a trash can lid, etc. Be creative and make it look like a pile of junk. Give the group just enough items to cross with but not so many that it is not a challenge. You want people to have to stand together on the same item, and you want them to have to pick up items and place them back down in order to get across.

Give the group the following rules before they begin their journey:
1. Once an item enters the junkyard it must maintain human contact at all times or it will float away (the leader moves it)
2. You can get objects back that have floated away if you use other objects to retrieve them.
3. If anyone touches the ground they have to return to the starting point and the group must make sure they can rejoin the junkyard "bridge."
4. No one can step across to the other side until each and every team member is standing on the "bridge."

Discussion Prompts

1. What was the most difficult part of this challenge?
2. Did anyone get frustrated at anytime? If so, how was it handled?
3. How did you feel about having to go back to the beginning if you touched the ground?
4. How do you feel when you have to start a project over because of a teammate's actions?
5. What are the advantages of starting over when working on a project with others?

Dominos Fall

Objective
To work together as a group on a project.

Group Size
2 or more

Materials
➲ None

Description
   Challenge the group to make a "dominos fall" out of a specified number of objects they find. The objects must fall in a dominos fashion where one knocks the next, which knocks the next, and so on. You may also do this as a competition of team versus team, or time the fall and see whose "dominos" take the longest time to finish falling.

Discussion Prompts
1. Did you use all the items that people found?
2. How much trial and error did you use for this activity?
3. How important is it to be willing to fail when on a team?
4. How does the failure help your team?

Open Up

Penny for Your Thought

Objective
For group members to affirm one another.

Group Size
4 to 20

Materials
➲ A large bag of pennies

Description
Give each person a handful of pennies. Each person must go up to each person in the group and say "a penny for your thought" and give them a penny. The person they approach must say something they like, admire, or value about the one who approached them.

Discussion Prompts
1. How do you feel about yourself after this activity?
2. How did you feel when you were telling others things you liked about them?
3. Which is harder, giving or receiving compliments? Why?
4. Would you like to do this type of activity more often? Why or why not?

Make a Recipe

Objective
For group members to share their thoughts on what makes a team work.

Group Size
2 or more

Materials
➲ Recipe cards (or 3x5 cards)
➲ Pens or pencils

Description
    Give each person a recipe card and a pen or pencil and ask them to write a "recipe for success." Depending on your group type, you may ask them to write a recipe for how to be a good team member, soccer player, good friend, etc. After everyone has spent time creating their own recipe for success, allow time for sharing.

Discussion Prompts
1. Did most people in the group come up with the same thing? Why do you think this is?
2. Do you feel you are following your recipe?
3. How could any of these "recipes" change your life?
4. Will you try to follow the "recipe"? Why or why not?

The Big Flower

Objective
For group members to think of and share positive attributes of the group as a whole and for each person to share his/her individual contributions to the group.

Group Size
4 or more

Materials
- A large sheet of paper
- Colored paper
- Marking pens
- Glue

Description
   Make a large flower on a piece of paper, and in the center of the flower write down things that the group members have in common (have the group give ideas). Give each person a piece of colored paper and have them cut out a flower petal for the flower. On the petal each person should write down something unique about him/herself and then glue it on to the big flower.

Discussion Prompts
1. Does the group have more things in common or more differences?
2. What benefits does a team get from having things in common?
3. What benefits does a team get from having individuals who are different?
4. Do you think anyone could have come up with more things for their flower petal than they did? If so, who and what?

Variation
- Have each person draw a flower petal onto the paper.

The Game of Life

Objective
To explore how people are feeling as individuals and as a part of the group.

Group Size
1 or more

Materials
- ➲ Large sheet of green paper
- ➲ White paper
- ➲ Colored markers
- ➲ Scissors

Description
On a large sheet of green paper, draw a simple football field in the middle as if it were in the middle of a stadium. Give each person a piece of white paper and ask them to think of the person at a football game who best represents them. You may be specific and ask them to think of the person they are most like in terms of their relationship with God, with their family, when at work, when on this team, etc. The person selected can be anyone from a player or referee to a fan, peanut man, blimp driver, usher, owner, etc. Each person should draw their character, cut it out, and glue it to the paper in relation to where they think it should be. After everyone is finished, have them explain why they chose what they chose.

Discussion Prompts
1. What did you learn about yourself while doing this activity?
2. What did you learn about the group or about other members of the group today?
3. Do you like being the person you are in the game of life or is there someone else you wish you could be? Why?

Encounter Clock Wise

Objective

For people to share their thoughts and feelings with other members of the group.

Group Size

13 or more

Materials

- ➲ One paper plate or piece of paper for each person
- ➲ Marking pens

Description

Ask each person to draw a clock on a piece of paper or on a paper plate. Then have them "make a date" with a different person for each hour on their clock, writing the name down for that hour. They can't have the same person twice and can't have two people in the same hour (unless there is an odd number of people).

Once each person has their clock filled up, give them a set amount of time to meet with each person. Call out the "hour" to begin their meeting. Have a list of questions for them to answer or topics you want them to discuss that pertain to the team.

Discussion Prompts

1. What did you learn from others today?
2. Did this activity make you talk with people you don't usually spend time talking to? If so, how did you feel about this?
3. How was this experience helpful for the team?

Life Map

Objective

For individuals to share with the group their goals and expectations in a nonthreatening manner.

Group Size

1 or more

Materials

- Paper
- Pens or pencils
- Optional: colored markers

Description

Give each person a piece of paper and something to write or draw with. Instruct the participants to draw a "life map" that starts at the point "you are here" and then travels along a road to their destination/s. The destination/s may be future goals, points in life, or future plans. There may be many forks in the road with different choices or paths to take, and there may be things along the way to see and do. Once each person has made a "life map" allow time for group members to share with the group.

Discussion Prompts

1. Are you excited about the map you have made for yourself?
2. Are there things you would like to see on your map but that you didn't put down? Why?
3. What did you learn about the others in the group?

Variation

- Have a group make one map that plots out the future course the group will take.

Bragging

Objective

For individuals to be proud of their own accomplishments and to verbally share these with the group.

Group Size

8 or more

Materials

➲ None

Description

Little kids are great at bragging "you know what I did…". This game gives everyone the chance to brag like a little kid. Divide the group into teams of about four each and have two teams face each other. Designate one team in each set of teams to start and someone on that team must brag about something they have done by saying "you know what, I…" and then follows this statement with a talent, attribute, or accomplishment they are proud of. Someone from the other team must answer back with words of bragging by the count of three or their team loses. Continue in this manner until one team in each set stops bragging.

Discussion Prompts

1. How did it feel to brag about yourself?
2. How did it feel to hear others brag?
3. Did you learn anything about yourself or about others?
4. How can complementing yourself help you?

Variation

➲ Do this with teams who work together and have them brag about things their team has accomplished.

Team Logo

Objective

For group members to work together to creatively share about the dynamics and positive traits of the group as a whole.

Group Size

2 or more

Materials

- Paper
- Colored markers

Description

Give the group a piece of paper and colored markers and ask them to create a logo that represents the entire group. Then have them explain it to you and explain how each person is represented in the logo.

Discussion Prompts

1. What aspects of your logo were easy? What aspects were difficult?
2. Would it have been easier or harder to create one for yourself?
3. Is there something you would like to add or subtract from your logo? Why?
4. Would you like this logo to always represent your group, or would you like a future logo to look different? Why?

Variations

- Break the group into smaller teams and have each team make up a logo about their team or about the entire group. Then have each team share their logo.
- Have each person make their own logo and then put them all on the same piece of paper. Discuss how they are similar or different and how each person adds unique qualities to the team.

Puzzle Collage

Objective
For each person to contribute to see how their attributes contribute to the group.

Group Size
4 to 16

Materials
- Large sheet of tag board
- Stack of old magazines
- Scissors
- Glue

Description
Cut a large piece of tag board into a puzzle. Give each person in the group a piece of the puzzle and ask them to make a collage of magazine pictures on their piece that represents who they are as a person. Allow time for each person to share what they made and then place it in the puzzle. You may glue the completed puzzle to another board and hang it on the wall.

Discussion Prompts
1. What similarities do you see in the members of this group?
2. What differences do you see?
3. Are there more differences or more similarities?
4. How does each unique person contribute to the larger group?

Bumper Sticker

Objective
For each person to share with the group how they see themselves.

Group Size
1 or more

Materials
- A blank bumper sticker (or piece of paper)
- Paper
- Colored markers

Description
Some craft magazines offer blank bumper stickers that can be colored with permanent makers and actually used on cars. For this activity you only need paper that is a pretend bumper sticker (you may want to cut them to size).

Have each person use symbols or words to create a unique bumper sticker that represents themselves. Then give each person another piece of paper and ask them to draw what they would look like if they were a car and to be prepared to explain. Allow time at the end of the activity for each person to share their sticker and car with the rest of the group.

Discussion Prompts
1. Did you learn anything about yourself as a result of this activity?
2. Did you learn anything about another member of the group?
3. Would you have made a different car to represent anyone else in the group than they chose for themselves? Why?

Tag Team Member

Objective

For each person to share with the group their individual strengths and positive traits that contribute to the overall success of the group.

Group Size

4 to 8 people per group

Materials

- Large sheet of paper
- Writing paper
- Pens or pencils
- Marking pens

Description

   Break the group into smaller groups of four to eight. Give each team one large sheet of paper, some writing paper, marking pens and a pen or pencil. Instruct the groups to make the "ultimate team member" by combining all of their best traits into one imaginary person. They need to give this "person" a name and draw a picture of him/her on the large sheet of paper with different attributes labeled. Then the group needs to write a story about this person. The story should highlight all of the amazing things their imaginary person can do with all of the awesome characteristics he/she has been given. Allow time at the end of the group time for each team to share their person and to read their story.

Discussion Prompts

1. If one person had all of your best traits would he/she be much better than any one person in your group?
2. How can you as a group member contribute to the team?
3. How does working as a team make things easier for each person?
4. What can you do as a team than you can't do by yourself?
5. What other attributes do you think you have to contribute to the team that were not mentioned in your story?
6. What other attributes do others in your group have that were not mentioned in your story?

Story Bracelet

Objective
For individuals to share their own "story" with the other members of the group.

Group Size
1 or more

Materials
- A variety of colored beads
- String, elastic, ribbon or anything that beads can be threaded on
- 3x5 cards or paper
- Pens or pencils

Description
Supply the group with beads and something to thread the beads on. Each person creates a bracelet using different colored beads to symbolize their experience when with the group. You may specify different aspects of their lives and ask them to pick a color for each aspect. For instance, one color may represent how they felt before being a part of the group, one color for how they feel when with the group, one color for the things they have gained from being with the group, and one for what they hope to see in the future as a result of being with the group. Or you may simply allow them to make up what different beads represent. Give each person a 3x5 card or piece of paper to write down his/her own "story" on.

Once everyone has completed a bracelet and written down its meaning, have them share with the group what they created and the story it tells.

Discussion Prompts
1. What did these bracelets have in common with each other?
2. Could we make one bracelet for the entire group that told a story? What would it look like and what story would it tell?

Variations

⮑ Have group members exchange bracelets after making them.

⮑ Instead of making a bracelet give the group small safety pins and small beads to make a beaded pin with instead.

Circle of Hands

Objective
To recognize the strengths and weaknesses of the group.

Group Size
6 or more

Materials
- Large sheet of paper
- Markers, crayons, pens or pencils

Description
Ask each person to trace his/her hand onto the large sheet of paper in order to form a large circle of hands. Have each person write their own name on the inside of their own hand. Ask the group to think of things that bring the group closer together and write these things inside of the circle. Outside of the circle write things that pull the group apart.

After the poster is created it may be used as a reminder of positive things group members can do to build up the group and also as a reminder of things to avoid.

Discussion Prompts
1. How can the group use this information?
2. Do you feel the group strives to become a close group? Why or why not?
3. How can this circle of hands help the group?

Flash Cards

Objective
For individuals to share how they see themselves within the group.

Group Size
1 or more

Materials
➲ One or more packs of word flash cards with pictures

Description
Spread the flash cards out on a table with the picture sides up. Ask each person to select one card that represents something that you specify: for instance, how each person is feeling at that time, how each person sees the group as a whole, what they hope to get out of being a part of the group, or anything else you think of.

Once each person has selected a card, have group members take turns sharing their card with the group.

Discussion Prompts
1. What do you think all of the cards selected say about the group as a whole?
2. Do you see anyone in the group differently now? Why or why not?
3. Do you think the whole group could agree on one card to select for the entire group?

My Neighbor

Objective

For group members to learn how others see them and to share how they are feeling.

Group Size

3 or more

Materials

➲ None

Description

Have the group stand or sit in a circle. Each person pretends to be the person on his/her right and states how s/he is feeling that day and describes what kind of day they have had (without asking the person). The person who was described gives a score of one to ten for accuracy and explains why before pretending to be the person on his/her right.

Discussion Prompts

1. Do you think you are easy to "read"? Why or why not?
2. Do you wish people knew more about what was going on in your life? Why or why not?
3. What clues do you give as to how you are feeling?
4. How can others knowing more about how you are feeling help you in your daily life?

The Open Book

Objective
For group members to work together to create a profile of the group as a whole.

Group Size
2 or more

Materials
- ➲ Paper
- ➲ Pens or pencils
- ➲ Colored markers

Description
Have the group make a book about the team, but with no story. Assign each person a different element of the book. For instance, one person thinks of a title for the book that reflects the group; another person writes the synopsis for the back cover. Other parts may include cover art, dedication, acknowledgments, table of contents, chapter titles, illustrations, etc. You can have them work together or separately. When everyone is finished, have them share their part of the book and put it together.

Discussion Prompts
1. What does this "book" say about the group?
2. Did you learn anything about the group from doing this activity?
3. If you could have a new title for a book about this group in a month or in a year, what would you hope the title would be?

More Team-Building Activities

Alphabetical List of Games

If you liked this book then you'll love Alanna's other team-building book Team-Building Activities for Every Group. The activities are all different from the ones found in this book but the book is laid out and presented in the exact same easy-to-use format!

107 interactive games and activities can be found in the pages of this easy-to-use book. Each game is fun, experiential, easy to lead, unique, and requires minimal resources. With 65 team challenges and 42 activities that help any team get to know one another, become comfortable with each other, and open up, there is something for every group.

If you work with youth, corporate groups, therapy groups, church groups, scouts, families, school groups, sports teams, at camp, or with any other group who must work together you will find helpful games and activities in this fun, energetic, and purposeful book!

~ ISBN# 0-9662341-6-2   192 pages   6"x9" ~

ADD ALANNA'S OTHER TEAM-BUILDING BOOK TO YOUR COLLECTION FOR ONLY $16!!

(Order form found on the last page of this book)

104 Activities That Build contains 104 games that encourage people to modify their behavior, increase interaction with others, start discussions, address issues and build relationships. This book covers the topics of Teamwork, Self-Esteem, Communication, Anger Management, Coping skills and Self-Discovery.

If you have a small group, large group or even one-on-one sessions there is something useful in 104 Activities That Build for you. Games that can be used in any setting with minimal resources and on any budget! It's more than pen/pencil worksheets; it's interactive and fun.

~ ISBN 0-9662341-3-8   272 pages   6"x9" ~

Add this book to your collection for only $24

Team Up

The team-building game you play with a group!

If your group liked the games in this team-building book, they will love the board game Team Up.

Team Up combines the fun of group initiative, problem solving and team-work activities with the simplicity of a creative new board game.

Team Up can be played in small teams of three or with a big group and teams as large as ten people each. Your team must work together each time it is your turn in order to win!

Team Up comes with a fold out game board, dice, playing pieces, therapeu-tic discussion sheets, and 200 different activities that challenge any group — physically, mentally, and individually — to work for the good of the team.

This is a fun game for camp groups, therapy groups, corporate groups, and scouts, and it is great for use in any classroom. Any group that wants to grow closer together and learn by taking risks and being challenged, while at the same time laughing a lot and having fun, will enjoy the game Team Up!

Team Up comes in a easy to use 3 ring binder with everything you need included.

YOU CAN ORDER IT NOW FOR ONLY $29!

Ages 8 to adult
8 to 60 people (you may play with as few as 6)

(Order form found on last page of this book.)

The wRECking Yard contains 104 more games and activities that are unique, fun and therapeutic. The book covers the topics of teamwork, self-esteem, self-discovery, leisure education, communication, anger management, and fitness.

Teachers, counselors, therapist, and youth workers across the country have found this book to be a valuable resource that is quickly growing in popularity!

ADD 104 MORE GREAT ACTIVITIES TO YOUR COLLECTION FOR ONLY $24!!

(Order form found on last page of this book.)

More Team-Building Activities

Book and Game Order Form

TITLE	PRICE	QUANTITY	TOTAL
Team -Building Activities for	$16	_____	_____
More Team-Building Activities	$16	_____	_____
104 Activities That Build:	$24	_____	_____
The wRECking Yard	$24	_____	_____
Team Up (board game)	$29	_____	_____

Washington State residents add 8% sales tax _____

Shipping: $4 (no matter how many items you order!) _____

TOTAL [_____]

Name _____

Address _____

City _____ State _____ Zip_____

Telephone (_____)_____

Payment Type: Visa _____ Master Card_____Check _____ PO_____
Card number

_____

Expiration Date _____/_____ Name on card_____

Order by Fax, Phone or Mail to:
Rec Room Publishing
PO Box 404
Richland, WA 99352
Phone 1-888-325-GAME or 509-946-7315
Fax 1-888-530-GAME or 509-943-7629

Web Page: www.gamesforgroups.com